REVEALED

ALEX KENDRICK and STEPHEN KENDRICK
with TROY SCHMIDT

REVEALED

Discovering Your
TRUE IDENTITY in CHRIST
for Teen Boys and Young Men

B&H
PUBLISHING
Nashville, Tennessee

978-1-5359-4988-0

Published by B&H Publishing Group
Nashville, Tennessee

Dewey Decimal Classification: 248.83
Subject Heading: SELF-REALIZATION / BOYS / TEENAGERS

1 2 3 4 5 6 7 · 22 21 20 19

CONTENTS

SECTION 3: WHAT HAVE YOU BECOME?

SECTION 4: WHERE ARE YOU GOING?

THE QUESTION
WE ALL ASK

Who are you?

It's a question you probably ask yourself all the time . . . I mean ALL THE TIME.

There's the self your parents see.

The self your friends like.

The self that gets made fun of.

The self you like or don't like—depending on the day.

And the self you try to be.

So who are you?

All the above? A little bit of each? Or maybe, none of them answer the question.

Have you ever thought about being a private investigator? A detective? A cold case solver? You may have been inspired by an investigator on television.

There are many different crime shows on TV, but the basic plot line of all of them is the same. A crime is committed. A brilliant team of investigators (all with special talents) come together to solve the mystery. Then there's a commercial break, an action scene involving cars, some talking, and another commercial. Finally, an amazing chase on foot through a crowded fruit market, where the crook is caught, and the heroes triumph.

Let's you and I take on a case together. It may not look exactly like the TV shows—I can't promise a heart-thumping car chase—but it certainly will be important, because this case involves something you should find very interesting—YOU.

HERE'S THE MYSTERY: WHO ARE YOU?

It's time to wrap some yellow police tape around yourself, because you're the one under investigation.

Many crime shows take place in big cities, but this kind of investigation is happening all the time, and everywhere.

Starting at an early age, guys just like you are asking themselves the same question: *Who am I?*

You can answer simply by saying: *I'm Hispanic, I'm level 92 on Fortnite, I get all A's,* or *I'm an athlete.* We usually stop there. But it's not that simple because what you really want to know is your IDENTITY.

Your identity is the foundation of all of you: past, present, future; internal thoughts and external behavior; actions, beliefs; your motivation and drive.

It's more than just saying "HI, MY NAME IS BILL SMITH." "Bill" is a name that identifies you. "Smith" separates you from other Bills. Then what? There are thousands of other Bill Smiths. Are they all the same? Of course their fingerprints and DNA are different, but more than that. They all look, sound, and act differently, with different dreams and different motivations. Their identities are unique. But, there are some similarities that we all share that can help us discover our unique identities.

In truth, there are four questions that need to be answered:

WHO ARE YOU?

WHAT HAVE YOU DONE?

WHAT HAVE YOU BECOME?

WHERE ARE YOU GOING?

The Bible has revealed the answer to all four of these questions, and in the end, will help you discover your true identity.

So why do we need to answer these questions? Because this crazy world will try to tell you who you are, and it won't line up with who you REALLY are. The world will lie to you at every turn, and as a result, you will struggle with doubt, hopelessness, and pain. But once you reveal the answers to who you are, then you can face the future with confidence and assurance.

Let's take on this case and find the answers.

The revelation will have eternal consequences.

SECTION 1

WHO ARE YOU?

CHAPTER 1

THERE'S BEEN A CRIME

Let's say you get out of school, walk to the parking lot to go home, and you discover . . .

Your car is gone.

Immediately you examine the scene, looking for clues.

There are cars all around, safe and intact, but not yours. No one else seems to be worried or missing their cars.

You begin to ask questions . . .

"Hey, has anyone seen my car? Did you see someone take it?"

Sadly, no one saw anything.

You look around for security cameras and spot one on a nearby lamppost that is pointed in the right direction.

You run inside to find Mr. Jenkins, the head of security for your school. As you tell him what's happened, he turns to his computer, pulls up the camera footage, and rewinds through time until he sees . . .

Mr. Ainsley! Wait . . . your fourth-period chemistry teacher stole your car?

You and Mr. Jenkins rush to his security golf cart. You fly down the road right into Mr. Ainsley's yard. You spot Mr. Ainsley in the garage, working on your car. Mr. Jenkins tackles Mr. Ainsley and ties him to a chair.

You click on a flashlight, shining the light in his eyes to let him know just how serious you are. And the interrogation begins.

You probably didn't ask Mr. Ainsley:

- How was your day?
- What did you have for lunch?
- Did I pass my mid-term?

No, you probably asked:

- Who do you think you are?
- Why did you steal my car?
- Do you regret what you've done?
- What are we going to do to fix this?

Any good investigator gets right to the point.

- IDENTITY: Who is this person?
- CONFESSION: Did they commit the crime?
- MOTIVE: Why did they commit this crime?
- REPENTANCE: Do they regret what they have done, and are they going to turn away from their life of crime?

In other words, mysteries can only be solved if the right questions are asked.

CHAPTER 2

THE BEST EYEWITNESS

We ask ourselves who we are and why we act a certain way all the time.

We question God, asking why He made us and what His purpose is in our lives.

Who you are is an important answer to know. It is crucial to so many life decisions and central to discovering your identity. Outside forces—friends, advertisers, social media (a.k.a. "the world")—are constantly trying to shape you into who they want you to be. And most of the time, they have hidden motives.

With so many thoughts and opinions bombarding you from the world—plus all the physical and emotional changes going on inside you—are you really the best person to answer that question?

As a young man at this stage in your life, your physical, mental, and spiritual state is in a perfect storm of transition. No matter how much we all hate to admit it, our perspectives are clouded by our limited view of life, and constant distractions.

For example, if you're in a car wreck, you have a front seat view of the accident, but you wouldn't see what was happening from the side, behind, below, or above. The best vantage point is from outside of the action.

Our internal eyes are limited too. Our age, skin color, and gender all adjust our perspective, seeing the same things differently from one another.

We can't see ourselves properly because our vision of ourselves has been clouded over time.

Plus, we tend to have tunnel vision, and we only see things straight ahead. That's why we need someone who sees us from the outside, from all directions, and throughout all time. Someone who knows our thoughts—and who knows the thoughts of others too.

More importantly, what if this person has plans for us, knows our potential, and has a standard to compare us to that is both fair and just?

Now who could that be?

CHAPTER 3

STARTING A PROFILE

INVESTIGATION PROFILE

NAMES

First name: _____

Last name: _____

Middle name: _____

Do you like your name? YES / NO

Why did your parents choose your name? _____

_____

_____

Do you know the meaning of your name? YES / NO

If YES, what is it? (If NO, look it up): _____

_____

Do you know the country where your name came from?

_____

What would you name yourself today if you could? _____

_____

Do you have a nickname? _____

Dad's name: _____

Mom's name: _____

Names of brothers and sisters: _____

_____

What are the names of your pets? _____

_____

What are the names of your closest friends? _____

_____

_____

LOCATIONS

What is the name of the town you live in? _____

_____

What state do you live in? _____

_____

What country do you live in? _____

_____

How many different places have you lived? _____

Name them: _____

_____

Where was your favorite place to live? _____

_____

Where would you live if you could live anywhere? _____

_____

What place/country do you want to visit in your lifetime?

_____

PERSONAL DETAILS

Eye color: _____

Hair color: _____

Ethnicity: _____

Height: _____

Weight: _____

Age: _____

How tall is the tallest member of your family? _____

_____

How short is the shortest member of your family? _____

_____

How tall do you want to be? _____

Who in your family do you most look like? _____

_____

FAVORITES

Color: _____

Food: _____

Restaurant: _____

Movie: _____

TV show: _____

Type of music: _____

Sport: _____

Sports team: _____

Board game: _____

Video game: _____

Car: _____

Phone app: _____

Social media: _____

Teacher: _____

Subject in school: _____

Animal: _____

Friend: _____

These details make you unique. It would be impossible for someone to have the same answers as you.

You are definitely not like anyone else. Your friends may like a lot of the same things. Your family probably matches you in a number of other areas. But no one is EXACTLY like you.

So does that mean that the mystery is solved? Is your identity revealed in these details?

No, that would be too easy.

What about the things that make you physically unique? Like your fingerprints?

No two people in the world have identical fingerprints. Not even twins. Your fingerprints develop in the womb, as your skin grows and stretches around your fingers, which are moving and grasping in those early months of development.

When we touch something we leave behind a sweat and oil deposit that our fingers press into and leave a lasting print. When someone commits a crime (without wearing gloves), crime scene investigators dust a light powder to highlight those fingerprints that are invisible to the naked eye. Those fingerprints go into a computer that analyzes and compares them to others in its database.

The FBI has a database called Integrated Automated Fingerprint Identification System (IAFIS), which has the names and fingerprints of around 70 million people. The entire science of fingerprints is called dactyloscopy (Dack-ti-loss-co-pee). It holds a lot of information, but doesn't hold the answer to your identity.

Your DNA is also unique.

Now I know you are not reading this book to help you on a biology test, but basically, DNA (**d**eoxyribo**n**ucleic **a**cid) is found in every cell of a person's body. This "code" is the same in every cell nucleus, but the code is unique only to that person, and replicates itself as new cells are created. These strands of DNA are made up of four chemical bases—adenine (A), guanine (G), cytosine (C), and thymine (T). Ninety-nine percent of those connections are the same for all humans, but it's that one percent that makes you, you.[1]

You are unique, from your head to your toes, from your fingerprints to your cells. There is no one like you. You are not a carbon copy; you are your own person.

And here's an important point—God made you that way. On purpose.

To better understand who you are, you need to know more about who made you and what He thinks about His creation.

The clues this gives you to your identity will astound you.

CHAPTER 4

COUNTING THE STARS

God knows every detail you listed in the chapter before—likes/dislikes, personal characteristics, locations, family, and so much more.

He's an expert on you. He could write a book about you. He could write THE book about you.

There are over 7.6 billion people on the earth,[2] and He knows you personally and completely.

God even knows how many hairs are on your head.

> *"So do not be afraid of them, for there is nothing concealed that will not be disclosed, or hidden that will not be made known. What I tell you in the dark, speak in the daylight; what is whispered in your ear, proclaim from the roofs. Do not be afraid of those who kill the body but cannot kill the soul. Rather, be afraid of the One who can destroy both soul and body in hell. Are not two sparrows sold for a penny? Yet not one of them will fall to the ground outside your Father's care. **And even the very hairs of your head are all numbered**. So don't be afraid; you are worth more than many sparrows."* (Matthew 10:26–31 NIV)*

How many hairs do humans have on their head? Go look into a mirror and start counting. Impossible, right? Here are some facts:

- Blondes have about 150,000 hairs.
- Redheads have around 90,000.
- If your hair is black or brown, you have about 110,000.[3]

So the average human head has 100,000 hairs. There are approximately 7,660,000,000 people on the planet.[4] That means God knows the current status of 7,660,000,000,000,000 hairs on human heads. (Yes, some people are bald, but this is an average.)

That's 7.66 quadrillion hairs that God knows quite well.

And that's just the humans. We haven't even gotten to the animals.

There are approximately 8.7 million species of animals on the earth. All the animals in all those species (the ones that have hair, and the ones that don't)—God knows them too.

But that's nothing.

He determines the number of the stars and calls them each by name. (Psalm 147:4 NIV)

There are nine planets in our solar system. Eight if you subtract Pluto.

They orbit around the sun. The sun is a star in the Milky Way.

The Milky Way has 200 billion more stars that are just like the sun.[5] Planets and moons orbit around each of them too.

God has a name for every one of them.

In addition to that, there are 100 trillion galaxies in the universe, each with 200 billion stars.

My calculator just exploded, but let's just say that's a lot of stars and a lot of names.

There are way more stars in the sky than hairs on human heads.

Every hair, every star . . . God knows them all.

So is it possible that He knows your true identity?

CHAPTER 5

QUESTIONING GOD

Job was a good man. He was living an honorable life, when all of a sudden, he lost everything.

- His kids
- His business
- His workers
- His crops

All gone. Then his health fell apart. Scratchy boils popped up and tore away his skin.

Job's friends showed up, letting him know they were there for him. Then all of a sudden, they turned on him; saying things like:

"You know this all happened because you've obviously sinned."

"You must have done something wrong. Confess."

"These bad things don't happen to good people."

God called Job a righteous man and you can't get a better endorsement than that. After thirty some chapters of his friends trying to convince Job he was a bad guy, God showed up to tell them this:

"I am God, and I will do what I please. Stop trying to figure Me out."

Job's friends got real humble, real fast.

That tends to happen when God shows up and speaks directly to someone. When the creator of the universe tells you you're wrong, you know it's true.

But, God uses this time to let them in on some amazing things about His power.

> *Then the LORD spoke to Job out of the storm. He said:*
>
> > *"Who is this that obscures my plans*
> > *with words without knowledge?*
> > *Brace yourself like a man;*
> > *I will question you,*
> > *and you shall answer me. (Job 38:1–3 NIV)*

God said to Job, "You have questions for me? Good. I've got some questions for you." You can feel the lump build in Job's throat as God asks Job in chapter 38:

- Did you make the earth and design its borders and foundations?
- Have you ever directed the day to start?
- Have you seen the deepest part of the ocean?
- Have you dropped in on death?
- Have you visited where light and darkness come from?
- Do you know how snow, lightning, rain, and ice work?
- Could you wrap up a constellation and throw it away?

When humans ask big questions like *Why did this happen?* and *What's going on?*, why does God respond by pointing out all the things humans don't understand? God's intention was not to make Job feel stupid, but to give Job and his friends a perspective on what they were dealing with.

"I've got so many things going on, Job. You have no idea how it's all working together."

It's like God is making a 7.6 billion-piece puzzle, and not only does He know what it will look like when it's finished, but He created the puzzle, and we are over here asking why He hasn't finished sorting out the edge pieces.

Check this out in Job chapter 39,

"Do you know when the mountain goats give birth?
Do you watch when the doe bears her fawn?
Do you count the months till they bear?
Do you know the time they give birth?
They crouch down and bring forth their young;
their labor pains are ended.
Their young thrive and grow strong in the wilds;
they leave and do not return.

"Who let the wild donkey go free?
Who untied its ropes?
I gave it the wasteland as its home,
the salt flats as its habitat.
It laughs at the commotion in the town;
it does not hear a driver's shout.

It ranges the hills for its pasture
and searches for any green thing.

"Will the wild ox consent to serve you?
Will it stay by your manger at night?
Can you hold it to the furrow with a harness?
Will it till the valleys behind you?
Will you rely on it for its great strength?
Will you leave your heavy work to it?
Can you trust it to haul in your grain
and bring it to your threshing floor? (vv. 1–12 NIV)

When's the last time you even thought about a mountain goat? Have you ever been traveling in the mountains and seen a mountain goat standing on a ledge, chewing on a gnarled root. In that moment, you look at the mountain goat, and you think, "I'm going to check up on that mountain goat every so often. I'll bring him food and make him a little shelter. I'll introduce him to a female mountain goat and maybe they'll have a nice family."

In all likelihood you've never seen a mountain goat. If you did, your thoughts probably haven't gone past, "Oh, that's a mountain goat."

The same goes for a pregnant deer, a crazy donkey, and a stubborn ox. No second thoughts about them unless you live on a farm.

We have trouble keeping up with our friends' birthdays, remembering our passwords, and the names of our teachers. But God's range of care for the world extends to mountain goats, pregnant deer, crazy donkeys, and stubborn oxen. He is quite familiar with each and every one of them.

God saw a mountain goat be born today, and He's keeping up with its progress and development for its whole life.

WHAT ARE SOME QUESTIONS YOU HAVE ASKED GOD?

_____

_____

HOW CAN YOU BE SURE GOD KNOWS ABOUT YOU?

_____

_____

WHAT DOES IT MEAN TO TRUST GOD?

_____

_____

CHAPTER 6

BEAUTIFUL FLAWS

Can we all admit something—ostriches are weird!

They have tiny heads and plump bodies, knobby knees and a goofy look on their faces.

They have wings and can't fly, but they can run around 40 miles per hour.

They bury their eggs in the sand and stick their head into the underground nest to see how their eggs are doing, which is probably why some people think they bury their heads in the sand when they're scared.

But ostriches aren't really the scared types. Ostriches are fighters.

God made these odd-looking birds and, guess what, He loves them.

God said this to Job in Chapter 39.

"The wings of the ostrich flap joyfully,
though they cannot compare
with the wings and feathers of the stork.
She lays her eggs on the ground
and lets them warm in the sand,
unmindful that a foot may crush them,
that some wild animal may trample them.

She treats her young harshly, as if they were not hers;
she cares not that her labor was in vain,
for God did not endow her with wisdom
or give her a share of good sense.
Yet when she spreads her feathers to run,
she laughs at horse and rider." (vv. 13–18 NIV)

Isn't it interesting how God describes the ostrich in these verses? And the ostrich sounds perfectly content being an oddball bird, flapping joyfully and laughing at the horse as she passes him with ease.

But the ostrich isn't perfect. In fact, God says she isn't very smart. The ostrich lays her eggs in the ground, even knowing that someone could come along and crush them. The ostrich doesn't seem to be a very good parent either and treats her kids harshly. Ostrich instincts do not promote the kind of close-knit parenting you see in animals like bears or sparrows who nest their children in the trees.

The ostrich:

- Looks funny.
- Can't fly.
- Can't build a nest.
- Is a poor parent.

But God loves her.

He loves His creation even knowing she is not perfect, at least by our standards. God doesn't focus on the flaws of the ostrich, but on the uniqueness of the ostrich.

LIKE AN OSTRICH, HOW ARE YOU UNIQUE?

_____

_____

LIKE AN OSTRICH, HOW ARE YOU FLAWED?

_____

_____

DO YOU THINK GOD STILL LOVES YOU?

_____

_____

God continued on with Job and described other creatures.

Ah, so majestic the horse, especially in battle, thumping its hooves and snorting excitedly as swords clash all around him.

Look at that hawk soaring gracefully in the air, perched high in the mountain tops, striking terror in the tiny animals as it swoops down for a meal.

God loves these creatures more, right? The perfect athletes. The Ivy League-accepted students. The handsome prom kings and queens parading before others.

Nope. He actually loves them the same amount as the rest.

God loves them, but He loves the bookworm too—and the class clown, the musician, the mechanic, the skater, and the quiet wallflower who sits in the back of the class hoping not to be seen. He loves them all.

It's the world who loves the hawks and horses.

It's God who loves the ostriches too.

CHAPTER 7

MONSTERS

Godzilla is a Japanese monster who originated in a 1954 film. He is a gigantic sea creature from the ocean floor, originally awoken by a nuclear bomb alarm clock—and boy, was he cranky!

He is two times taller than the tallest skyscraper and equal in size to many mountains. His long destructive tail can wipe out three city blocks, and his radioactive fire breath can burn down entire cities with one sneeze.

His name is a compilation of two Japanese words that mean *gorilla and whale*, describing his power, size, and strength.

For humans, Godzilla is the scariest monster we could ever imagine.

For God, Godzilla is a chihuahua.

After God unleashed these two previous chapters on Job, He said this:

> *"Will the one who contends with the Almighty correct him?*
> *Let him who accuses God answer him!" (Job 40:2 NIV)*

In other words, "Do you really think you know enough to be able to correct Me?" Job, by now, cowered in a corner in the fetal position, hiding under a table with a blanket over his head answered.

> *Then Job answered the LORD:*
> *"I am unworthy—how can I reply to you?*
> *I put my hand over my mouth.*
> *I spoke once, but I have no answer—*
> *twice, but I will say no more." (Job 40:3–5 NIV)*

Job, shaking and shivering, said, "I'm done. You win." But God wasn't done. In 40:8–14, God asked Job these questions:

- Would you discredit My justice? (v. 8)
- Would you condemn Me to justify yourself? (v. 8)
- Do you have an arm like Mine? (v. 9)
- Do you have a voice like Mine? (v. 9)
- Can you adorn yourself with glory and splendor? (v. 10)
- Can you unleash your wrath and humble the proudest person? (v. 11–13)

Job (wisely) said nothing in response, but his answers would be *No, No, No, No, No, No.*

Then in verses 15–24, God described, well, Godzilla.

- Strong and muscular (v. 16)
- A tail like a mighty tree (v. 17)
- Unbreakable (v. 18)
- Fearless (v. 23)
- Uncapturable (v. 24)

This was the Behemoth and is the only place it is mentioned in the Bible. So what was the Behemoth?

BlueLetterBible.com says the original Hebrew translation of the word could be "an extinct dinosaur, a Diplodocus or Brachiosaurus, exact meaning unknown."[6] It offers other animals that it could be, like a water-ox or hippo.[7]

It's a big land creature. The biggest one around at the time.

Then in chapter 41, God described to Job another creature. Meet the Leviathan.

- A fierce, struggling fighter (vv. 1–2, 8–10)
- Strong limbs (v. 12)
- Impenetrable exterior (v. 13)
- Scary teeth (v. 14)
- Shields on his back (v. 15)
- Flames from its mouth (vv. 19–21)
- Strong (vv. 22–27)
- Unstoppable (vv. 28–29)

BlueLetterBible.com says the original Hebrew translation of this word is a "sea monster, dragon, large aquatic animals, perhaps the extinct dinosaur, plesiosaurus."[8] It offers two suggestions for this creature—a crocodile and a dragon.[9]

Okay, I know immediately a dozen questions are going through your mind:

- Did Job hang out with dinosaurs?

- Did dragons exist?
- Is the Loch Ness monster for real?

Scientists, scholars, and theologians debate those things in their spare time, but I want to keep focused on the topic at hand.

Godzilla is what would happen if the Leviathan and the Behemoth had a baby, an enormous land and sea monster, described even down to the fire breath and the big ol' tail.

And if Godzilla were real, God would put him on a leash and have him completely house broken in seconds.

That's the strength of the God you worship.

A God who can tame any situation.

A God who is not afraid of any monsters in your life, whether hiding under the bed, in the closet or in your future.

That God has your back . . . and He made you.

CHAPTER 8

WHO IS GOD?

So, private investigator, you've examined the evidence in Job; what is your conclusion?

Job came to his own conclusions in chapter 42.

- God can do all things (v. 2)
- Nothing God wants can be stopped (v. 2)
- God has plans (v. 3)
- God hears our prayers (v. 8)
- God restores us, sometimes twice as much (v. 10)
- God blesses us (v. 12)

This God who knows all our hairs, names all the stars in the galaxy, knows what all the mountain goats are doing, who created a wonderfully goofy ostrich, and could make a Tyrannosaurus Rex his pet, THIS GOD knows you and cares about you.

He can do anything He wants and chooses to pay attention to you.

Who is God? Your creator, your designer, your protector, your sustainer.

You are who God says you are because He made you.

CHAPTER 9

WHO ARE YOU?

If you're like most people, you probably have questions about yourself constantly running through your mind.

- Who am I?
- Why am I this way?
- Why do I live where I live?
- Why do I have this family?
- Why do I look this way?

Good questions.

Let's look first at what the Bible reveals.

In Genesis 1, God created the whole universe. Everything in it, from light to lemurs, stars to starfish, the mountains to mockingbirds.

Then, as a fitting finale—a satisfying conclusion to the story—God created the stars of the show. Human beings.

Then God said, "Let us make mankind in our image, in our likeness, so that they may rule over the fish in the sea and the birds in the sky, over the livestock and all the wild animals, and over all the creatures that move along the ground." (Genesis 1:26 NIV)

God made us in His image and gave us a job. Rule over this earth!

We rule!

WHAT DOES IT MEAN TO RULE THE EARTH?

We have responsibility. We must protect. We must build. Create. Just like God does. It's our job and it's been built into us.

So God created mankind in his own image,
in the image of God he created them;
male and female he created them. (Genesis 1:27 NIV)

How are we supposed to rule? We're supposed to rule over the earth the way God rules over the earth, because He made us in His image.

What does it mean to be created in God's image? Does God have a face, arms, torso, legs, feet? Jesus said,

"God is spirit, and his worshipers must worship in the
Spirit and in truth." (John 4:24 NIV)

If God is spirit, then He does not have a human body. Jesus came to earth as a human. Right now, Jesus has a human (resurrected, glorified) body, but the other members of the Trinity do not have human bodies.

So if we're made in the image of God, then we must reflect something else about God. His characteristics.

LIST THE FIRST FIVE CHARACTERISTICS OF GOD THAT COME TO MIND.

_____

_____

_____

_____

_____

If that's God and you're made in His image, then you have the potential to reflect all those characteristics.

LIST ALL THE CHARACTERISTICS IN YOU THAT REFLECT GOD.

_____

_____

_____

_____

_____

Look at that list. Look at the potential you have and who you could be.

You are defined by who made you, and according to your creator . . . you are good. At least, good in the sense that because you're His creation, you have incredible value and purpose.

God saw all that he had made, and it was very good. (Genesis 1:31)

I mean, VERY good.

CHAPTER 10

WHAT DO YOU THINK?

You have between 50,000 to 70,000 thoughts a day.[10]

There, that was one.

And that was another.

That's between 30 to 40 thoughts a minute.

God knows every one of those thoughts.

In a world of over 7 billion people, that's . . .

350,000,000,000,000 thoughts per minute

350 quadrillion thoughts.

What do you think of that? (That's another thought . . .)

In Psalm 139, David talked about this incredible side of God. He's our X-ray, ultrasound, and CT Scan—constantly investigating our minds and bodies.

You have searched me, Lord,
and you know me.
You know when I sit and when I rise;
you perceive my thoughts from afar.
You discern my going out and my lying down;
you are familiar with all my ways. (vv. 1–3 NIV)

God knows what position you're sitting in right now. Sitting in a coffee shop, slouching on the couch, standing at the bus stop, laying in your bed reading this book.

He knows every thought in your head and every word out of your mouth.

Before a word is on my tongue
you, LORD, know it completely. (v. 4 NIV)

Men say about 7,000 words a day. Women say about 20,000 words a day.

Every thought . . . every movement . . . every word . . .

You hem me in behind and before,
and you lay your hand upon me.
Such knowledge is too wonderful for me,
too lofty for me to attain. (vv. 5–6 NIV)

There's no place you can go on this earth where God can't find you. Even if you hide in the dark.

Where can I go from your Spirit?
Where can I flee from your presence?
If I go up to the heavens, you are there;
if I make my bed in the depths, you are there.
If I rise on the wings of the dawn,
if I settle on the far side of the sea,
even there your hand will guide me,
your right hand will hold me fast.
If I say, "Surely the darkness will hide me
and the light become night around me,"

even the darkness will not be dark to you;
the night will shine like the day,
for darkness is as light to you. (vv. 7–12 NIV)

That's right. God has radar, sonar, and infra-red vision.

God can do this because He has the unlimited capacity to attain and retain all the information from over 7 billion souls at the same time.

Our computers have some pretty incredible memory capacity these days.

- Gigabyte (GB) = 1,073,741,824 bytes
- Terabyte (TB) = 1,099,511,627,776 bytes
- Petabyte (PB) = 1,125,899,906,842,624 bytes

A byte is approximately one bit of information.

God has petabytes of petabytes of memory. He can simultaneously see all and know all—everywhere at every time, even before it happens.

You aren't so lost that God can't find you.

You aren't so confused that God can't remind you.

You aren't so insignificant that God doesn't pay attention to you.

WHAT DO YOU THINK OF YOU NOW?

CHAPTER 11

MADE ON PURPOSE

Somewhere on just about everything you buy, there's a manufacturer's label giving the serial number, make, model, and place of construction/assembly of the item.

You can tell a lot about an item by looking at where and how it was made.

Some items are assembled with cheap labor while under difficult conditions. Others are made with high standards and highly skilled labor.

WHERE WERE YOU MADE?

Before you name the city where you were born, read more of Psalm 139:

For you created my inmost being;
you knit me together in my mother's womb.
I praise you because I am fearfully and wonderfully
    made;
your works are wonderful,
I know that full well.
My frame was not hidden from you
when I was made in the secret place,
when I was woven together in the depths of the earth.

Your eyes saw my unformed body;
all the days ordained for me were written in your book
before one of them came to be. (vv. 13–16 NIV)

You were made by God in your mother's womb (His design, manufacturing, and distribution center). During your formation from egg to baby, God actively supervised the process, approving all the materials.

NOW IT'S TEST TIME!

(Don't worry—it's easy because this test is all about YOU.)

Answer these questions according to Psalm 139:

1. Who created you? (v. 13)
2. How were you put together? (v. 13)
3. What does *fearfully made* mean? (v. 14)
4. What does *wonderfully made* mean? (v. 14)
5. How well did God oversee the process? (v. 15)
6. Who approved your final design? (v. 15)
7. How well was your future put together at that time? (v. 16)

ANSWERS:

1. God created your inmost being.
2. You were knit together. Knitting is a slow process that requires concentration and hands-on work. Every stitch is carefully designed and tied

together. You weren't carelessly cranked out in an automated factory—you were carefully planned.

3. The word *fearfully* has a lot of meanings in the original Hebrew, but the best definition that applies here is "awesomely and with astonishment."

4. *Wonderfully* means "distinct, separate, unique." You are not a carbon copy. You are unique.

5. Your frame was not hidden from God. He saw the whole process of your creation in the womb. Nothing got past His eyes.

6. You were made secretly (in your mom's womb) or maybe the word *privately* fits here, away from outside influencers.

7. All your days were ordained. God had a plan for you, and He purposed that plan beginning at birth. You either choose that plan or reject it as you grow up.

How well did you do on the test? Many are not aware how incredibly they were made. They think babies are just flying out of the factory before God has a chance to inspect them. There are bound to be some that slip by undetected— the broken, disassembled, the unloved, right? NOPE.

Large nose? LOVED BY GOD!

Big? LOVED BY GOD!

Short? LOVED BY GOD!

Can't see? LOVED BY GOD!

Can't walk? LOVED BY GOD!

Low IQ? LOVED BY GOD!

Not the culture's definition of attractive? LOVED BY
GOD!

Stutter? LOVED BY GOD!

Freckles and zits? LOVED BY GOD!

Apparently God's standards of beauty and perfection are much different than ours.

Every one of these truths from Psalm 139 apply to every person ever born. They don't just apply to the strong and athletic; the cool and handsome.

God doesn't make mistakes. He created you, and He loves you just the way you are.

CHAPTER 12

THE SUM OF ALL THOUGHTS

Let's summarize what we have revealed about WHO YOU ARE.

1. God is incredibly powerful, eternal, very detailed, and involved in everything that ever existed.
2. He made you.

Does that about sum it up?

If our awesome God made you—WHAT DOES THAT MAKE YOU?

We'd love to ask Him, right? You'd want to know all those questions we posed earlier.

- Who am I?
- Why am I this way?
- Why do I live where I live?
- Why do I have this family?
- Why do I look this way?

What would He say? Before we answer, let's look at the rest of Psalm 139.

How precious to me are your thoughts, God!
How vast is the sum of them!

Were I to count them,
they would outnumber the grains of sand—
when I awake, I am still with you. (vv. 17–18 NIV)

God has many thoughts in His head.
Remember those numbers:

- 7.6 billion people
- 350 quadrillion thoughts

We have one thought and God has 50 million thoughts at the same time.[11]

What's the point here? The answer isn't simple or easy or explainable in one sentence.

Or . . . maybe it is.

BECAUSE

Have your parents ever said that to you?

"Dad, why are we going there today?" Dad: "Because."

"Mom, why are we having that for dinner again?" Mom: "Because."

Are your parents lazy and tired and don't want to answer? Maybe. Or are they hiding the real reason for their answer? Maybe.

The answer "Because" means "Because I said so" which also means "I'm in charge—trust me." It's a statement made by someone in authority who has a reason, or a complete summary of reasons, to the questions of who, what, when, where, why, and how, but they feel telling you is unnecessary because they want you to trust them.

Now we must stop and ask ourselves, why are we asking God these questions?

Do we want to be in charge and tell God what to do?

Yes, that's a pattern consistent to human beings since the beginning of time. So we must drop our pen and paper and turn the investigation back on ourselves. Take that bright spotlight and shine it in our own eyes. Psalm 139 has more to reveal:

> *Search me, God, and know my heart;*
> *test me and know my anxious thoughts.*
> *See if there is any offensive way in me,*
> *and lead me in the way everlasting. (vv. 23–24 NIV)*

Then wait for the results to print out.

Pray this to God right now . . .

Fully scan all my thoughts and tell me how my heart is doing. Go deep, look hard, give me the most thorough stress test imaginable. What's wrong in there, God? What parts are faulty? I want to run efficiently for eternity.

NOW LISTEN.

WHAT DID GOD SAY?

_____

_____

CHAPTER 13

WHO ARE YOU?

Our first investigation is winding down. We asked the question, "Who am I?" and looked at Scripture to reveal the answer.

Satisfied? One more story to help us understand the answer.

There was a prophet named Jeremiah who God gave a difficult task. He told Jeremiah to confront the religious leaders of Jerusalem and tell them their actions were going to bring down the city and end the nation. It was not going to be easy. Powerful, prideful people don't like to be told they're failures. Jeremiah would be mocked, beaten, and imprisoned during those years.

In Jeremiah 1, God announced His plan and purpose for Jeremiah by saying this:

> The word of the LORD came to me, saying,
>
> > "Before I formed you in the womb I knew you,
> > before you were born I set you apart;
> > I appointed you as a prophet to the nations."
> > (Jeremiah 1:4–5)

God said to Jeremiah, "I know who you are because I made you." He knew Jeremiah's name, address, and career path.

God designs and shapes us in our mother's womb, but He also creates us with a purpose. There's something He wants us to do.

If you knew your whole life right now, how would you react?

No, it's better that you don't know the answers all at once, but trust God to reveal them to you slowly over time.

Jeremiah doubted when he got the news that he was going to be a prophet.

> *"Alas, Sovereign L*ORD*," I said, "I do not know how to speak; I am too young."*
>
> *But the L*ORD *said to me, "Do not say, 'I am too young.' You must go to everyone I send you to and say whatever I command you. Do not be afraid of them, for I am with you and will rescue you," declares the L*ORD*. (Jeremiah 1:6–8 N*IV*)*

Jeremiah learned to accept the BECAUSE answer. God said, "Trust Me, just go where I tell you to go, do what I tell you to do. Don't be afraid. I'll protect you."

Jeremiah said OKAY and went ahead.

Would you?

The answer to WHO AM I? isn't simple. There isn't one easy answer or a true/false question. There are multiple answers to who you are. Your purpose fits into the plan of 50 quadrillion thoughts. You have a role in everything going on in this earth for all time.

And you're not too young to discover it.

You are here for a reason.

Who are you? You are fearfully and wonderfully made.

Now that we know who you are, let's go to the crime scene.

SOMEONE IS DEAD!

SECTION 2

WHAT HAVE YOU DONE?

CHAPTER 14

COMMITTING A CRIME

Back to Mr. Ainsley, the car thief. Mr. Jenkins takes him inside to find out the truth.

Now that the coast is clear, you look around the garage.

You look on Mr. Ainsley's workbench. Wait, are those your keys? You feel your pockets. Empty.

Then you remember, you pulled out the keys during chemistry looking for a piece of gum. You must have forgotten them, and Mr. Ainsley found them.

You then take a look at what Mr. Ainsley was doing when you found him. Your car is up on a jack. Your tires were low and the brakes were making terrible noises.

You approach the car and look at the tires. Full and ready to go. One tire is off and clean new brake pads are in place.

Right then, you get a text. It's Mr. Jenkins. *The police are on their way.*

Time's running out. To do a thorough investigation, you need to talk to the culprit and discover his motive. You have a bunch of questions for him. You fly into the house.

We established in the last section that you are an amazing person, developed by an incredible God. This God loves you, knows you, and watches you every moment.

You should be speechless.

So how do you respond to God's love? Worship and surrender? Offerings and service? No, like everyone else, you sin and disobey. How's that for appreciation?

God sees your sin, and He grieves.

And do not grieve the Holy Spirit of God, with whom you were sealed for the day of redemption. (Ephesians 4:30 NIV)

Why does God grieve? He knows that your sin separates you from Him, now and forever. God doesn't want that. He made you and loves you. He wants a relationship with you. That's why God gave you freewill, so you could choose to love Him.

Come near to God and he will come near to you. Wash your hands, you sinners, and purify your hearts, you double-minded. Grieve, mourn and wail. Change your laughter to mourning and your joy to gloom. Humble yourselves before the Lord, and he will lift you up. (James 4:8–10 NIV)

God wants us to grieve over our sins. But, as humans, we choose what we think is best for ourselves. That's what sin is, choosing what we think is best for ourselves, rather than following what God says is best for us.

Why do we choose to sin? And how did it all begin?

If we understand the truth behind sin, maybe it will help us keep it from happening again.

CHAPTER 15

THE ORIGINAL CRIME SCENE

The scene of a crime is an important component to understanding and solving the crime.

If a crime occurs at home, there are different motivations, emotions, and consequences than if a crime happens at work, church, or school. A detective will suspect different people depending on the location.

But let's go back and look at the first crime ever committed. The first time someone broke the law; God's law.

The garden.

God created us in His image, and He wanted us to love Him like He loves us, as a living, breathing, thinking, deciding human being.

God created this beautiful home called Earth and put man in the most beautiful place on Earth called the garden of Eden.

The garden of Eden was perfect and stunning. It had everything a person would need.

The LORD God caused to grow out of the ground every tree pleasing in appearance and good for food, including the tree of life in the middle of the garden, as well as the tree of the knowledge of good and evil. (Genesis 2:9)

God also made two unique fruit trees: the tree of life and the tree of the knowledge of good and evil. But these trees were much more than mere fruit trees.

Fruit from the tree of life meant eternal life and living in a relationship with the eternal God. In Him is life and if we live in a loving relationship with God, then we get eternal life. Choosing that tree and consuming its content meant life for Adam.

Fruit from the tree of knowledge represented the understanding of evil through choice. We understand good because we've chosen good things. We understand evil because we've chosen bad things.

God wanted Adam to choose life and not experience the consequences of choosing evil, so He named these trees after those choices.

The LORD God took the man and placed him in the garden of Eden to work it and watch over it. And the LORD God commanded the man, "You are free to eat from any tree of the garden, but you must not eat from the tree of the knowledge of good and evil, for on the day you eat from it, you will certainly die." (Genesis 2:15–17)

That was the entire law—one rule. Seems pretty simple, right? Wouldn't you love to live in a place with just one rule—do whatever you want, Adam, but don't eat from that one tree, the tree of knowledge of good and evil.

But wait, why did God even make this one rule? Why even put that knowledge tree there in the first place?

Four reasons.

1. **Rules create choice**. You can choose to follow the rule or not.
2. **Rules measure obedience**. You can choose to obey the rule or not.
3. **Rules establish authority**. You can choose to obey the rule-maker or not.
4. **Rules show love**. You can choose to love someone by obeying or not.

You probably have rules in your house you follow because you're told to and you're afraid of the consequences, such as being grounded or having your computer, phone, or Xbox taken away.

What if you chose to follow those rules because you love the one who gave them to you? That's right. You express your love, not only through flowers and cards, but by serving and doing what you're asked to do.

If you follow the rules because you hate the consequences, then you are only thinking of yourself. If you follow them to show your love for the one who gave them to you, you are thinking of others first.

But if you don't listen at all, what are you saying then?

Truth is, you're saying this: "I don't care what you tell me to do. I'm more important than you." Or even, "I hate you."

It may seem like just taking the trash to the curb on Thursdays, but it communicates something much larger.

Love the LORD your God and keep his require-ments, his decrees, his laws and his commands always. (Deuteronomy 11:1 NIV)

In God's world, you show your love to Him through obedience.

God created this one rule so . . .

1. Adam would understand choice.
2. Adam had the opportunity to obey.
3. Adam would know who is in charge.
4. Adam had a way to show his love for God.

God said don't eat from one fruit tree in a garden of many other fruit trees. Not a hard rule to follow . . . right?

WRONG!

God created us with the wonderful characteristic called freewill where we can choose what's best, but we can also choose what's worst. God doesn't want a population of robots. He wants a deep, meaningful, interactive relationship with people who choose to love Him back.

That one choice meant death.

This day I call the heavens and the earth as witnesses against you that I have set before you life and death, blessings and curses. Now choose life, so that you and your children may live and that you may love the LORD your God, listen to his voice, and hold fast to him. For the LORD is your life, and he will give you many years in the land he swore to give to your fathers, Abraham, Isaac and Jacob. (Deuteronomy 30:19–20 NIV)

CHAPTER 16

EVERYTHING HAS CONSEQUENCES

There are some crazy rules out there.

In Arizona, you need a permit to feed garbage to a pig.[12]

In California, you can own frogs for frog jumping contests, but if one dies, you can't eat them.[13]

In Southington, Connecticut, you can't use Silly String outside your home.[14]

In Indiana, you can't catch fish with your bare hands.[15]

In Minnesota, you can't chase a greased pig.[16]

It doesn't matter if you think the rule is crazy. It's the law and there are consequences that come with breaking it.

If you do a crime, you must do the time. The consequences for breaking one of these state laws isn't likely to be the death penalty.

But in the garden of Eden, eating from the wrong tree meant death.

God made a woman for the man for companionship. Adam named her Eve. One day a snake arrived in the garden. This slithering, slippery, malicious nemesis was none other than Satan. He's not so much the Crime Committer, but more like the Crime Boss, influencing others to do his dirty work.

So how does Satan get Eve and Adam to commit the crime and break the rule?

He confuses. *"Did God really say, 'You can't eat from any tree in the garden'?"* (Genesis 3:1). Satan got the woman to rethink and question what the rule really was.

He lies. *"No! You will not die,"* the serpent said to the woman (Genesis 3:4). Actually, God did say they would die if they ate the fruit. Don't believe the deceiver or you will die!

He tempts. *"In fact, God knows that when you eat it your eyes will be opened and you will be like God, knowing good and evil"* (Genesis 3:5). Satan told Eve there was a better life out there and she should go get it for herself.

In only five verses, Satan influenced our downfall. Adam and Eve both chose to disobey the one and only law in the whole world.

When the Law Giver showed up in the garden, Adam and Eve did what criminals still do today. They hid. We're guilty of that too. We hide our sins hoping no one will discover them. Do we really think we can hide from God? As we learned in the last section, that's impossible.

Like we all do, Adam and Eve blamed others for their crime. We hate to take responsibility. God, disappointed, laid out the consequences . . . the death sentence.

- Genesis 3:14–15—He cursed Satan and separated him from the life he once had.

- Genesis 3:16—He sentenced Eve to painful child-birth.
- Genesis 3:17–19—He sentenced Adam to hard work, and eventual death, returning to the dust in the ground.
- Genesis 3:23-24—God removed humanity from the garden so they could no longer eat from the tree of life.

What's the common theme of all these punishments? Separation. Punishments today still have to do with separation.

Fines separate your money from your wallet.

Community service separates your time from your schedule.

Prison separates you from your life and family.

Solitary confinement separates you from other people.

Execution separates you from this earth.

But your iniquities have separated you from your God; your sins have hidden his face from you, so that he will not hear. (Isaiah 59:2 NIV)

And the sentence for the crime of eating from the forbidden tree was separating us from paradise and separating us from God. Death means no life. If God is life, then our sin separates us from the life-giver, God. If we choose sin, we choose death.

The tree of life is no longer within reach.

Pretty serious consequences, but Adam and Eve had the choice to say no to Satan's confusion, lies, and temptations. And they chose what they wanted for themselves.

After all this happened in Genesis 3, humanity learned its lesson, right?

Wrong! The next story in Genesis 4 is yet another crime. Murder! A brother murders his brother and it's Adam and Eve's only two sons.

Cain got jealous of his brother Abel's offerings to God. Thinking God loved Abel more, Cain planned to kill him. But God came to Cain, saying . . .

"Why are you furious? And why do you look despondent? If you do what is right, won't you be accepted? But if you do not do what is right, sin is crouching at the door. Its desire is for you, but you must rule over it." (Genesis 4:6–7)

"Don't do it, Cain! Do the right thing and I'll accept you. Sin crouches at the door of your heart and wants to get in. It wants to bring you down and destroy you. Don't do it! Rule over it! Control your choice!"

Can't you hear God's voice? What does Cain do in response? He murders his brother anyway.

God rolled out the consequences and separated Cain from the rest of his family.

Sin is in our very nature. We were born to sin.

Indeed, I was guilty when I was born;
I was sinful when my mother conceived me.
(Psalm 51:5)

We cannot NOT sin. We will sin. Separation is in our future.

The heart is more deceitful than anything else,
and incurable—who can understand it?
I, the LORD, examine the mind,
I test the heart
to give to each according to his way,
according to what his actions deserve. (Jeremiah 17:9–10)

One sin and you are declared guilty.
And you are guilty.
Just admit it . . .

CHAPTER 17

THE LIST OF CRIMES

Here is a list of fifty rules found in the Bible. Circle/Check the ones you've broken.

1. Do not have other gods besides the real God.
2. Do not make an idol for yourself.
3. Do not misuse the name of the LORD your God.
4. Remember the Sabbath day and keep it holy.
5. Honor your father and your mother.
6. Do not murder.
7. Do not commit adultery.
8. Do not steal.
9. Do not give false testimony (lie) against your neighbor.
10. Do not covet (desire) your neighbor's house (wife, animals, or stuff).
11. No evil thoughts
12. No sexual immoralities
13. Don't be greedy.
14. No evil actions
15. Don't deceive people.
16. Don't self-indulge.
17. Don't envy.

18. Don't slander.

19. Don't have pride.

20. Don't be foolish.

21. Don't criticize.

22. Don't boast.

23. Don't be arrogant.

24. No moral impurity

25. No sorcery

26. No hatred (like prejudice)

27. No strife (don't cause anger)

28. Don't be jealous.

29. No outbursts of anger

30. No selfish ambitions

31. No dissensions (divisions)

32. No factions (cliques)

33. Don't get drunk.

34. Don't wildly party.

35. Don't love money.

36. Don't demean others or be verbally abusive.

37. Don't disobey your parents.

38. Don't be ungrateful.

39. Don't be unholy.

40. Don't be unloving.

41. Don't be out of control.

42. Don't be brutal.

43. Love what is good.

44. Don't be a traitor.

45. Don't be reckless.

46. Don't love pleasure.
47. No homosexuality
48. Don't gossip.
49. Be trustworthy.
50. Show mercy.

Now, we're going to complicate things. Jesus said,

*"You have heard that it was said to our ancestors, **Do not murder**, and whoever murders will be subject to judgment. But I tell you, everyone who is angry with his brother or sister will be subject to judgment. Whoever insults his brother or sister, will be subject to the court. Whoever says, 'You fool!' will be subject to hellfire."* (Matthew 5:21–22)

*"You have heard that it was said, **Do not commit adultery**. But I tell you, everyone who looks at a woman lustfully has already committed adultery with her in his heart."* (Matthew 5:27–28)

Does that mean what it sounds like it means?

Yes. God is concerned about where your heart is, and when you lust after another person, then you are guilty of committing that sin in your heart.

Let's remember something we learned earlier. If you break one rule, you are guilty, regardless of whether you've kept the other rules.

Did you make it past #1—Do not have any other gods before me?

- Have you ever worshiped (put in the position of #1 in your life) another god, or a sport, or a video game, or a girl, or a friend, or yourself?

Guilty.

Why even go on to #2? You're dead at #1.

So is sin a serious offense in God's eyes?

Look at what Jesus said,

"If your right eye causes you to sin, gouge it out and throw it away. For it is better that you lose one of the parts of your body than for your whole body to be thrown into hell. And if your right hand causes you to sin, cut it off and throw it away. For it is better that you lose one of the parts of your body than for your whole body to go into hell." (Matthew 5:29–30)

Did Jesus mean that it's better for you to cut off your hand than to steal from your dad's wallet? He did. Did Jesus mean that it's better for you to cut off your foot than to kick your little brother in the face? He did.

Sin is serious, and God doesn't want you committing the crimes.

Why?

1. It hurts you.
2. It hurts others.
3. It encourages others to hurt themselves.
4. It makes life difficult.
5. It ruins families.

6. It separates people from God.

7. It causes people to choose hell.

8. It keeps people from meeting Jesus.

Should I go on?

God loves you, and He knows that doing things His way is the only way and the best way to live.

It's clear God loves you. Now who do you love? God . . . or the world?

> *Do not love the world or the things in the world. If anyone loves the world, the love of the Father is not in him. For everything in the world—the lust of the flesh, the lust of the eyes, and the pride in one's possessions—is not from the Father, but is from the world. And the world with its lust is passing away, but the one who does the will of God remains forever. (1 John 2:15–17)*

It all starts with lust (an intense desire for something) and pride (thinking you're the most important thing that ever lived).

- LUST OF THE FLESH—physical pleasure, sex, drugs, alcohol
- LUST OF THE EYES—coveting, envying, greed, pornography
- PRIDE IN POSSESSIONS—desiring the world more than God

Remember that lying, deceitful snake in the garden? Those lies still work today only now Satan doesn't use fruit, but the things of the world. He confuses, lies, and tempts us to substitute sex, money, clothes, fame, or popularity for God's truth. Exchanging doing what's right for what we think we want. And if you take his bait . . .

You are a dead man walking.

CHAPTER 18

DEAD MAN WALKING

When a person is heading to be executed, people yell out "dead man walking." The man is certainly alive, but he's walking to his death, so he's as good as dead.

The saying applies to us too. If we've committed any of the sins mentioned in the last chapter, then we are guilty and sentenced to die. We are still physically alive, but walking through life to our eventual death, and separation from God forever.

Imagine you are sitting in prison, awaiting your execution. What thoughts go through your head?

You might blame other people.

"I had a terrible lawyer."

"That judge had it out for me."

"The police planted the evidence."

"I was falsely accused."

Remember the scene in the garden of Eden? When God discovered that the crime happened, what did Adam and Eve do? Blame.

The man replied, "The woman you gave to be with me—she gave me some fruit from the tree, and I ate."

So the Lord God asked the woman, "What is this you have done?" And the woman said, "The serpent deceived me, and I ate." (Genesis 3:12–13)

"It's the woman's fault!"

"It's the snake's fault!"

Many even try this one: "God, it's your fault! You made me this way!"

Blame is the game in prison and in life.

While this dead man walking scene is pretty extreme and few people on the earth are actually aware of their death date and time, we really are no different. If you are a human being on this earth and you've sinned, your death date awaits. The clock is ticking. You may not know the day and time, but you know a day and time is coming.

And you were dead in your trespasses and sins in which you previously lived according to the ways of this world, according to the ruler of the power of the air, the spirit now working in the disobedient. We too all previously lived among them in our fleshly desires, carrying out the inclinations of our flesh and thoughts, and we were by nature children under wrath as the others were also. (Ephesians 2:1–3)

In prison, we separate the prisoners from their life and family. At the moment we sin, we are separated from God and a time will come at our actual death when we will be separated from God forever, with no chance of parole.

Don't you know that the unrighteous will not inherit God's kingdom? Do not be deceived: No sexually immoral people, idolaters, adulterers, or males who have sex with males, no thieves, greedy people, drunkards, verbally abusive people, or swindlers will inherit God's kingdom. (1 Corinthians 6:9–10)

Sinful people don't get into heaven. Why?

Heaven is where the Life-Giver lives and where those who choose life go.

Those who choose death (sin) go exactly where they want to go—away from God.

Heaven is where the holy, sinless One lives. God has committed no sin and has never been contaminated by sin. If He allows sinful people into His house, then He is approving sin and allowing death into the place of life.

So let's go back to you sitting on death row awaiting your execution. What thoughts go through your mind?

Blame? This is no time to blame, but time to accept responsibility. Admit you are a sinner.

List your good deeds? Many try to impress God by doing all kinds of nice things. They want God to see them and forget all the bad things they've done. But it doesn't work that way.

All of us have become like something unclean,
and all our righteous acts are like a polluted garment;
all of us wither like a leaf,
and our iniquities carry us away like the wind.
(Isaiah 64:6)

Our "righteous acts" or "good deeds" are like a polluted garment, also translated into a "bloody rag." If you received a bloody rag, you wouldn't think, "Oh, this is a perfectly good rag. I could still use it." No, you would throw it out!

Good deeds don't take the stains out of our lives.

Sitting there in prison, you must admit that you are a sinner. In fact, you must admit your sinfulness is so bad, that you're addicted to it. A slave to sin.

Jesus responded, "Truly I tell you, everyone who commits sin is a slave of sin. A slave does not remain in the household forever, but a son does remain forever." (John 8:34–35)

Admit you are a slave to sin. You choose it all the time.

Admit that you are where you are because you chose it for your life.

This prison you find yourself in is one you chose.

CHAPTER 19

YOUR OWN PRISON

If you could design your own prison, would it have Wi-Fi? Video games? A 70-inch TV? A library of books? A cell phone? Unlimited visitation time for your friends? A king-sized bed? Food delivered to your prison cell? Doors and windows you can shut for privacy or see out when you want?

Wouldn't really be "prison," would it? So let's look at it this way—say you are confined to your room . . . how long would that be fun and amazing?

One day—yes!

One week, two, three weeks—okay . . . getting old.

A month, two months, six months—LET ME OUT!

HOW WOULD YOU FEEL AFTER A YEAR CONFINED TO YOUR BEDROOM?

_____

_____

Not so much fun. What's missing one year later that replaced the wild excitement of day one?

Freedom.

Yes, you are free to do whatever you want to do in that confined space, but you can't experience anything outside that confinement. After a while those walls that you once considered your playground now become your prison.

You ask yourself, "Is this all there is? Is this all life was meant to be?"

Prison is a place where one's freedom is contained. Prison is a place where you are separated from what life has to offer.

The beginning of this chapter asked you to think about your personally designed prison. Truth is, we've been designing our own prisons since birth. Sin designs our prison cells. The more you sin, the more confined the cell. Every sin moves the walls in closer and closer, until it's a closet and you can't breathe.

Sin separates you and confines you, walling you in on all sides.

> *But your iniquities are separating you*
> *from your God,*
> *and your sins have hidden his face from you*
> *so that he does not listen. (Isaiah 59:2)*

Your sins get so bad that God can't even look at you anymore. That's what that verse says. When God hides His face and doesn't even listen to you any longer, you are in deep trouble.

Here's where many people want to blame God: "How could He do such a thing as ignore me? Sure, I'm not perfect, but who is? This is a mean God who won't listen to my prayers!"

Who caused this? Who really is to blame? God didn't cause your sin. You chose to sin. You designed your prison. God made you to be free.

You are confined to your prison, waiting on death row, and there's no one to blame but yourself.

What if it were forever? I mean . . . forever.

READ THESE VERSES ABOUT HELL. CIRCLE THE DESCRIPTIONS.

"But the subjects of the kingdom will be thrown outside, into the darkness, where there will be weeping and gnashing of teeth." (Matthew 8:12 NIV)

"They will throw them into the blazing furnace, where there will be weeping and gnashing of teeth." (Matthew 13:42 NIV)

"If your hand causes you to stumble, cut it off. It is better for you to enter life maimed than with two hands to go into hell, where the fire never goes out." (Mark 9:43 NIV)

For if God did not spare angels when they sinned, but sent them to hell, putting them in chains of darkness to be held for judgment. (2 Peter 2:4 NIV)

The devil who deceived them was thrown into the lake of fire and sulfur where the beast and the false prophet are, and they will be tormented day and night forever and ever. (Revelation 20:10)

But the cowards, faithless, detestable, murderers, sexually immoral, sorcerers, idolaters, and all liars—their share will be in the lake that burns with fire and sulfur, which is the second death. (Revelation 21:8)

What common themes do we see here?

- Fire—hot where things are reduced to ashes, meaningless, destructive
- Weeping—sadness, despair, mourning, sorrow, loss
- Gnashing of teeth—worry, struggle, regret
- Darkness—lost, directionless, insecurity, fear
- Chains—confinement, no freedom
- Torment—hurt, pain

Hell is the ultimate, final prison.

Imagine this confinement FOREVER. Not one week or three months or six years, but always and never ending.

Why? Why would God allow this?

He allows it because people chose it and continue to choose it. On Earth, people choose to ignore Him and outright disobey Him, making it very clear they want nothing to do with God. So why would God allow them into His presence forever if they don't want to be there?

God gave us the freewill to choose Him or not, and He honors that freewill at death.

Heaven is the place everyone should choose. Heaven is the complete opposite of hell.

And I heard a loud voice from the throne saying, "Look! God's dwelling place is now among the people, and he will dwell with them. They will be his people, and God himself will be with them and be their God. 'He will wipe every tear from their eyes. There will be no more death' or mourning or crying or pain, for the old order of things has passed away." (Revelation 21:3–4 NIV)

No more crying. No more death. No more mourning. No more pain. Just God . . . 24/7.

Heaven is described as a place of light, joy, praise, freedom, refreshing water, beautiful landscapes, singing. Why? Because God is there.

Hell is hell because God isn't there. He knows how horrible it is and He wants to free people from its torment.

Then the Lord knows how to rescue the godly from trials and to keep the unrighteous under punishment for the day of judgment, especially those who follow the polluting desires of the flesh and despise authority. (2 Peter 2:9–10)

As a God who is perfect in justice—people getting the punishment they deserve—He must punish people who pursue the "polluting desires of the flesh and despise authority." We want those kind of people locked up on Earth, right?

But He is also perfect in mercy and wants to free people from punishment on the day of judgment. To do so, God must make sure someone pays the price for each and every sin.

So He gave us the best possible criminal defense lawyer. His Son.

CHAPTER 20

YOUR ONLY DEFENSE

You might have heard a prisoner on TV say, "I have a right to make one phone call."

Is that true? Yes, in America the police will allow you to make a phone call, maybe two for good behavior. They will take your phone away when they frisk you, so either you need to have a phone number memorized or they can pull out your phone to get a number.[17]

You also have a right to legal representation (a lawyer). You don't have to talk to the police without a lawyer present. All that comes from a case called *Miranda v Arizona*, which went all the way to the Supreme Court. Here's what police officers say when they make an arrest. (Let's hope you never have to hear this.)

> You have the right to remain silent. Anything you say can and will be used against you in a court of law. You have the right to an attorney. If you cannot afford an attorney, one will be provided for you. Do you understand the rights I have just read to you? With these rights in mind, do you wish to speak to me?[18]

So that first call you make should be to a lawyer or to someone who can help find you a lawyer. You need someone on your side who knows the law inside and out. You can hire one or the court can appoint one to you (at no charge).

Some people think they can defend themselves. That's dangerous. They watched too many law shows and think they know all the court terminology.

You'll just end up looking foolish.

When it comes to your court date with God, as you plead your case to Him about why He shouldn't sentence you to ultimate, final prison (hell), who will defend your case?

Yourself? Okay. How well do you know the law? It's complicated and scary, one false move could doom you forever.

Most people representing themselves love to list all their good deeds.

"Your honor, I was a good person on Earth. I went to church on Easter and Christmas. I prayed to God, every now and then. I gave money to good causes. I read the Bible once in a while. I was nice to people and animals. I let people merge onto the highway. I gave a homeless man a quarter. I told my mom that I loved her."

Listing your good deeds is a distraction from all your bad deeds. What if the opposition decided to respond by listing all your bad deeds?

Do you have a month to spare?

You need a good lawyer to come to your defense. But what makes a good lawyer?

You probably can think of a list of expected qualities of a lawyer—smart, good speaker, tough, knows the law, excellent listener, sharp dresser. All definitely important when it comes to being a lawyer.

How about this—he's real, like he actually exists. We have in our mind what a lawyer should look like and act like, but most lawyers aren't all those things.

Jesus is the only defense you need. He's real, and He's free.

The apostle John hung out with Jesus for three years while Jesus did ministry in Israel with His apostles. John testified that he witnessed Jesus firsthand.

What was from the beginning, what we have heard, what we have seen with our eyes, what we have observed and have touched with our hands, concerning the word of life—that life was revealed, and we have seen it and we testify and declare to you the eternal life that was with the Father and was revealed to us—what we have seen and heard we also declare to you, so that you may also have fellowship with us; and indeed our fellowship is with the Father and with his Son Jesus Christ. We are writing these things so that our joy may be complete. (1 John 1:1–4)

John considered it a joy to tell others about Jesus!

Now that we know Jesus is real, what can He do for us as our legal representation? The word used in the Bible is *intercede*. Intercede means to stand in the gap for us. In legal terms, there's the accused or defendant on one side and the law or justice on the other. The lawyer stands between the two to help the defendant.

Jesus intercedes between us and the Judge, God the Father.

> *My little children, I am writing you these things so that you may not sin. But if anyone does sin, we have an advocate with the Father—Jesus Christ the righteous one. (1 John 2:1)*

John calls Jesus our advocate. An advocate speaks for us, pleading our case to God. There's also another person in the courtroom—an accuser. This one stands up in court and points out our sins, reminding the court how terrible we are. The name "devil" actually translates to mean "accuser and slanderer." The devil wants to focus on all your bad stuff.

Your lawyer doesn't listen to the lies of the devil. Your lawyer listens to the truth.

Your lawyer is truth.

> *"You will know the truth, and the truth will set you free." (John 8:32)*

By getting to know Jesus—your advocate, your defender, the real deal—you then know truth.

Here's another qualification you probably didn't think about when looking for a lawyer—he loves you. If the lawyer loves you, he's going to work extra hard to defend you and free you. You don't see many lawyer billboards saying . . .

"If you need help, call me. I love you."

"Because when the world hates you, know that I'll always love you."

Yeah, sounds weird.

But not if your lawyer is Jesus.

For God loved the world in this way: He gave his one and only Son, so that everyone who believes in him will not perish but have eternal life. (John 3:16)

This famous verse tells us that not only does Jesus love us enough to die for us, but the judge loves us too. That's extremely good news. The lawyer and the judge love us!

Here's another qualification for a lawyer that probably didn't come to mind either—sacrificial. How many lawyers do you know who would represent you in court, and then take on the punishment for your crime?

The lawyer pays the fine.

The lawyer goes to jail for you.

The lawyer switches places with you and goes to death row to die for you.

Probably not one lawyer on the planet would ever do that.

He made the one who did not know sin to be sin for us,
so that in him we might become the righteousness of God.
(2 Corinthians 5:21)

Jesus, our advocate, went to court for us; and when we were pronounced guilty of sin, He offered to assume the penalty of that sin for us—in essence wiping the sin from our record and putting it all on His record.

At that moment we become RIGHT with the legal system. We're GUILTY, but the punishment of our guilt has been paid for by our lawyer, our advocate, Jesus the Son of God.

Jesus paid for our sin by shedding his blood and dying on the cross. If our sins are paid for, then our record is clean. If our record is clean, then our sins are wiped away.

Jesus isn't our lawyer to get us off on a technicality. He isn't there to lower our sentence or make some emotional plea that sways the judge.

Jesus is there to tell us to confess and allow Him to take on the consequences.

If we walk in the light as he himself is in the light, we
have fellowship with one another, and the blood of Jesus
his Son cleanses us from all sin. If we say, "We have no
sin," we are deceiving ourselves, and the truth is not in
us. If we confess our sins, he is faithful and righteous to
forgive us our sins and to cleanse us from all unrigh-
teousness. If we say, "We have not sinned," we make him
a liar, and his word is not in us. (1 John 1:7–10)

Truth is you are a sinner, so start by confessing and saying, "I DID IT! I'M GUILTY! I'M A CRIMINAL! I'M A SINNER!"

Our lawyer knows we're guilty. The judge knows we're guilty. Our accuser knows it too, yet he doesn't want us to accept Jesus' plea bargain. The devil wants us to think we're so bad that nobody can save us. He's a liar. Don't listen to him.

The apostle John reaffirms this.

> *Everyone who commits sin practices lawlessness; and sin is lawlessness. You know that he was revealed so that he might take away sins, and there is no sin in him. Everyone who remains in him does not sin; everyone who sins has not seen him or known him.*
>
> *Children, let no one deceive you. The one who does what is right is righteous, just as he is righteous. The one who commits sin is of the devil, for the devil has sinned from the beginning. The Son of God was revealed for this purpose: to destroy the devil's works. Everyone who has been born of God does not sin, because his seed remains in him; he is not able to sin, because he has been born of God. This is how God's children and the devil's children become obvious. Whoever does not do what is right is not of God, especially the one who does not love his brother or sister. (1 John 3:4–10)*

Let's summarize what John teaches us about God's legal system.

- You broke God's law by sinning.
- Jesus can take away the sin from your record.
- Jesus is sinless and can clean your record.
- Once Jesus does that for you and you remain close to Him, He will help you not to sin.
- You are right with God (righteous) by doing what is right.
- If you commit sin, you're following the devil.
- Jesus wants to destroy what the devil caused.
- Either you are born of God or born of the devil—you choose.

If you choose Jesus as your lawyer, He makes a promise to you:

And this is the promise that he himself made to us: eternal life. (1 John 2:25)

You will not die and be separated from God. You will live with Him eternally.

But time is running out.

They just called your name.

You're heading to court.

It's judgment day.

CHAPTER 21

SAVED

This is the day. You're walking to court to receive your final judgment.

There's a heavy darkness in the air as you realize this will be your last day on Earth. With every step, the chains clank reminding you of your crime. They are wrapped around your wrists, securing your arms, and wrapped around your ankles, keeping you from running away.

Your sins are the chains, and you are a prisoner because of your choices.

Every step of the way, your lawyer walks by your side.

He reminds you of your final option, your only hope to be set free. It isn't an easy option, but necessary for the death sentence to be removed from your life.

"First you need to know that **everyone sins and falls short of the glory of God**.[19] It's not just you being singled out. Everyone is in the same position when it comes to sin."

You're not the only sinner on this earth. The rules here apply to everyone. No exceptions.

Your lawyer continues, "But there's some good news." You perk up. **"God proves his own love for you in that while you were still a sinner, Jesus died for you**.[20] Your sin did not stop His love for you. In fact, He chose to die for you, whether you would accept His death or not."

Your mind can't believe what you're hearing. Many who knew you stopped calling when they found out that you were arrested, and here's Jesus, who knew ALL YOUR SINS, still trying to connect to you, even willingly to die for you. That proves how much He loves you.

The lawyer puts his arm around you. "**For the wages of your sin is death, but the gift of God is eternal life in Christ Jesus your Lord.**[21] You earned your death like you would earn your wages on a paycheck. But God is offering you a gift. Wages and a gift are very different."

Wow, he's right. You work for wages, but you don't work for a gift. A gift is freely given out of love, with no strings attached. And while you've earned death, you're being given a free gift of eternal life.

Your lawyer opens a door and allows you to step through. The courtroom is only a few dozen feet away.

"**Therefore, there is now no condemnation for those in Christ Jesus.**[22] If you want to be 'in' Christ and allow Christ to live in you, nobody can condemn you of your sins. Nobody! Jesus loves you. **I know for sure that neither death nor life, nor angels nor rulers, nor things present nor things to come, nor powers, nor height nor depth, nor any other created thing will be able to separate you from the love of God that is in Christ Jesus our Lord.**[23] Once He saves you and you truly, sincerely, humbly, deeply accept that gift of salvation, you are genuinely saved."

The courtroom door is only an arm's reach away. Your fate is on the other side. What do you do?

You can't escape the sentencing. They have all the evidence. The fingerprints. The DNA. The testimonies. The past crimes you committed. Plus, the judge knows every thought, every word you've ever said. He has all the hairs on your head counted.

He knows you're guilty!

Maybe, you think, you can blame others? Then you remember that didn't work for Adam and Eve. Maybe you can hide. But how can you hide from God?

You stop in your tracks. Sweat dripping down your face. Your death sentence awaits three feet ahead on the other side of the door.

The guard pushes you ahead, but you resist. You turn to the lawyer. "Tell me, advocate, what do I do, what do I say? I don't have much time!"

Your lawyer leans in and whispers into your ear. The words are so powerful, they wipe out any other sound in the room.

"If you confess with your mouth, 'Jesus is Lord,' and believe in your heart that God raised him from the dead, you will be saved."[24]

Suddenly a final shove from the guard pushes you into the courtroom. You stumble ahead five awkward steps and fill the room with obnoxious clanks, causing everyone in the room to turn and look at you. They all know what's about to happen and their faces look sad for you.

Except one. The accuser. He smiles. He points at you and announces:

"There he is. The rotten criminal himself. This guy is the worst. There's no way he'll stop sinning. He can never be good enough for God to accept him. God has high standards, but this one, he'll never earn the right to enter heaven. What a disgrace. He deserves death."

You hear those words and the accuser is right. You are a hopeless sinner.

What can you say? The accuser makes a good case. You turn to your lawyer for one last piece of advice, something that will help you, save you.

Your defense lawyer smiles. He knows just what to say: **"For everyone who calls on the name of the Lord will be saved."**[25]

Then you remember all those things your lawyer said.

. . . free gift . . .

. . . eternal life . . .

. . . no condemnation . . .

. . . nothing can separate . . .

. . . saved . . .

It doesn't all make sense, but it gives you hope. You'll just have to believe and have faith with what information your lawyer told you.

You rush the judge at his bench and fall on your knees.

"I confess! I'm a sinner! I've earned my death! I've fallen short! I confess right here and right now that I need Jesus. I trust Him as my Lord. He's God. He loves me, and He died for me. He paid for my sin on the cross! I also believe Jesus rose again from the grave because He's God and death can't hold Him down. I choose Jesus! I cry out in the name of the Lord to be saved! Please forgive me!"

You begin to weep, your head falling into your hands. You said all you could say, all that came to mind. You hope it was enough.

You look up from your tears and see your accuser. For some reason, he looks beaten, exhausted, dejected. He falls into his chair, throwing his hands up.

You turn to your lawyer. He's smiling, nearly laughing with joy. Nodding His head—yes, yes, yes.

Then you turn slowly to the judge. You're afraid to see His face. Is He looking at you or away from you in shame?

He's looking right at you, and He's smiling too.

For a moment that seems to take hours, He lifts His gavel and slams it down, announcing, "You're free to go! The punishment has been paid."

Suddenly, miraculously, the chains are taken off your wrists and your ankles.

Your lawyer wraps His arms around you, "You're saved! Your record is now clean!"

HAVE YOU PRAYED A PRAYER LIKE THAT BEFORE? YES / NO

ARE YOU SAVED—A CHRISTIAN—A BORN-AGAIN BELIEVER? YES / NO / NOT SURE

Praying that prayer can mean life or death.

We must cross-examine ourselves and ask two more questions before we can truly know our identity in Christ.

CHAPTER 22

HOW DO I TRULY REPENT?

Ever watch *Cops* or one of the camera-following-an-officer-around TV shows? What happens every time a person gets caught doing a crime?

1. They deny.
2. They blame.
3. They run.
4. They confess.

The first three happen all the time. The fourth option is rare. People try every possible way to get out of a situation before admitting they were wrong.

The word *repent* in the Bible means to be sorry and turn around. Is that it? It's as simple as that?

We've seen many people come on TV and say they're sorry. Sometimes it's heartfelt with tears and everything. Other times it feels like a speech they rehearsed or a performance worthy of an Oscar.

We know, because admit it, we've done it too. We've said, "Hey, sorry, Mom" only to get out of any more trouble. Saying sorry is a way to move on, to hope that this won't have any more serious repercussions.

What does it mean to truly repent in God's eyes? Is it as simple as saying some words, reading a prepared speech, quoting a Scripture, and God stamps your papers—FORGIVEN?

No way. God knows your heart. He knows a sincere repentance when He hears one.

It begins with acknowledging that you are a sinner.

If we say, "We have no sin," we are deceiving ourselves, and the truth is not in us. If we confess our sins, he is faithful and righteous to forgive us our sins and to cleanse us from all unrighteousness. If we say, "We have not sinned," we make him a liar, and his word is not in us. (1 John 1:8–10)

Admitting that you are a sinner is admitting that you are wrong. But it goes deeper than that.

In the book of Romans, where we traced our walk toward salvation, Paul the apostle also wrote this:

There is no one righteous,
*   not even one.*
There is no one
*   who understands;*
there is no one who seeks God.
All have turned away;
*   all alike have become worthless.*
There is no one who does
*   what is good,*
not even one.

Their throat is an open grave;
they deceive with their tongues.
Vipers' venom is under their lips.
Their mouth is full of cursing
     and bitterness.
Their feet are swift
     to shed blood;
ruin and wretchedness are
     in their paths,
and the path of peace
     they have not known.
There is no fear of God
     before their eyes. (Romans 3:10–18)

According to this passage, each of us must admit:

- I'm not right.
- I've done dumb things.
- I haven't sought God in my life.
- I've turned away from Him.
- I'm worthless without Him.
- I don't do any good.
- My words are deadly and bitter.
- I deceive people.
- I hurt people.
- My life is ruined and wretched.
- I cause wars and division.
- I don't fear God.

That's a lot deeper than just saying "Hey, I'm sorry God. I'll do better next time." No, this is crying out in pain over your sinfulness.

The word *repent* in the Bible does mean "to be sorry," but it adds another element to it: "to be grieved" and "to change one's mind."

Repenting is hating your sin, despising what it's done in your life, and crying out for forgiveness, solely throwing yourself on the mercy of God's court.

David in the Bible got lost in his power and began to believe all the positive press about himself. He got distracted by wealth and women, taking a soldier's wife to bed, then murdering the woman's husband when David got her pregnant. A prophet named Nathan pointed the sin out to David, saying God knew what he did. David then repented.

> *Then I acknowledged my sin to you*
> *and did not conceal my iniquity.*
> *I said, "I will confess my transgressions to the LORD,"*
> *and you forgave the guilt of my sin. (Psalm 32:5)*

David knew confession began the process of forgiveness. He could not imagine lying or justifying his sin any longer. In sorrow and pain, David acknowledged who he was.

Psalm 51 is David's confession and plea.

Read it slowly and CIRCLE the words that express his sin.

Be gracious to me, God,
according to your faithful love;
according to your abundant compassion,
blot out my rebellion.
Completely wash away my guilt
and cleanse me from my sin.
For I am conscious of my rebellion,
and my sin is always before me.
Against you—you alone—I have sinned
and done this evil in your sight.
So you are right when you pass sentence;
you are blameless when you judge.
Indeed, I was guilty when I was born;
I was sinful when my mother conceived me.

Surely you desire integrity in the inner self,
and you teach me wisdom deep within.
Purify me with hyssop, and I will be clean;
wash me, and I will be whiter than snow.
Let me hear joy and gladness;
let the bones you have crushed rejoice.
Turn your face away from my sins
and blot out all my guilt.

God, create a clean heart for me
and renew a steadfast spirit within me.

Do not banish me from your presence
or take your Holy Spirit from me.
Restore the joy of your salvation to me,
and sustain me by giving me a willing spirit.
Then I will teach the rebellious your ways,
and sinners will return to you.

Save me from the guilt of bloodshed, God—
God of my salvation—
and my tongue will sing of your righteousness.
Lord, open my lips,
and my mouth will declare your praise.
You do not want a sacrifice, or I would give it;
you are not pleased with a burnt offering.
The sacrifice pleasing to God is a broken spirit.
You will not despise a broken and humbled heart, God.

In your good pleasure, cause Zion to prosper;
build the walls of Jerusalem.
Then you will delight in righteous sacrifices,
whole burnt offerings;
then bulls will be offered on your altar.

Now read it again. This time UNDERLINE what David wants God to do in response to his confession.

David believed his confession would:

- Unlock God's grace, love, compassion
- Wash away his guilt

- Cleanse him of sin
- Restore joy and gladness to his life
- Create a new heart
- Strengthen his spirit
- Give him opportunities to teach others about God
- Save him

Do you want that in your life?

Do you despise your sinfulness and desire a new relationship with God where you can live a life that pleases Him?

Really?

Are you at a point in your life where you can't go on unless something changes in your life? Do you realize you are far from God and you must destroy the separation you've caused?

David later said this:

Search me, God, and know my heart;
test me and know my concerns.
See if there is any offensive way in me;
lead me in the everlasting way. (Psalm 139:23–24)

Do you give God permission to search you, test you, discipline you, correct you of any offensive actions and thoughts so you can be on the path to eternity, where you will meet God face-to-face?

David was truly repentant, and he said this:

How joyful is the one
whose transgression is forgiven,
whose sin is covered!
How joyful is a person whom
the LORD does not charge with iniquity
and in whose spirit is no deceit! (Psalm 32:1–2)

Repentance is a good thing, but it's hard to do. How good is it? When you repent, a party breaks out in heaven.

I tell you that in the same way there will be more rejoic-
ing in heaven over one sinner who repents than over
ninety-nine righteous persons who do not need to repent.
(Luke 15:7 NIV)

Genuine, sincere, heartfelt repentance is difficult, but in heaven it's seen as the beginning of life, another heavenly resident, someone they can get to know forever, a new brother in Christ.

It's a good thing. It'll make you feel better, but, better yet, you become better.

Now, onto the next big question . . .

CHAPTER 23

HOW DO I KNOW I'M FORGIVEN?

If you imagined that scene in the courtroom where God considered all the sinful evidence against you and had over-whelming cause to convict you, but instead of judgment and prison, your confession unlocked God's gracious response to allow Jesus' death on the cross to pay for all your sins—then the emotion you experience should be joy.

The joy of salvation, of being set free.

However, if you're like most people, you doubt and you wonder, "Wait, that was too good to be true. Are my sins truly forgiven?"

Rest assured . . . you are forgiven.

Jesus died on the cross *as our sin.*

He made the one who did not know sin to be sin for us,
so that in him we might become the righteousness of God.
(2 Corinthians 5:21)

His death on the cross washed us of all sin. Not a hint of stain is on our record.

"Come, let us settle this,"
says the LORD.

"Though your sins are scarlet,
they will be as white as snow;
though they are crimson red,
they will be like wool." (Isaiah 1:18)

So while we may think we're good with God up to the point of our confession, what about all those moments afterward? Do we have to keep confessing and repenting?

Yes, but this is to continue walking in fellowship with Him.

To understand how far God distanced us from our sins, we must answer the question—how far is the east from the west? If we know that, then we will understand how far God removed our sins from us.

The widest distance in the United States from the east coast to the west coast is approximately 2,800 miles. That's about the distance from New York City to Los Angeles.[26] That's far, but not far enough.

The width of Russia, the longest country from east to west, is almost 5,700 miles.[27] Almost twice as wide. While 5,700 miles is a long distance from east to west, it's still reachable. If you drove 24 hours a day at 70 miles per hour, it would only take you around four days to drive border to border in Russia. Not far enough.

The minimum distance from Earth to Mars is 33.9 million miles.[28] It's far, but reachable. Six rovers have landed on the surface of Mars (so far). Though difficult to get there, still, it's attainable.

That's why Psalm 103 is so comforting. East is east, and west is west. They never reach a point of connection. Wherever you are in this world, there's always an east and always a west. It's like saying my sins are as far away as right from left, or up from down.

Also, when you accept Jesus Christ as your Savior, you move into a new relationship with God. You are now family. God is your father and Jesus calls you His brother.

You have a father here on Earth (and hopefully have a good relationship with him). You've probably made him mad by doing something stupid. But did that stop you from being his son? No. There may be distance, but the family title was not removed. You are your father's son, and your relationship is restored back to health when you get things right with him.

Family dynamics are complicated on Earth. Not all earthly fathers live up to ideal standards. God wants to be that perfect father to you. He has compassion on you instead of condemning you. While your behavior may disappoint Him, and maybe anger Him, you're still His son, and He will treat you as a loving Father, even if that includes discipline (Hebrews 12).

However, if you mess up and sin (and you will), then you should repent. Asking for forgiveness works on Earth to bring people closer together. It's the same way in heaven. You don't have to ask for forgiveness to get saved over and over, but you should ask for forgiveness to repair the distance your sins put between you and God.

We also know that we are forgiven because we've been healed.

He himself bore our sins in his body on the tree; so that, having died to sins, we might live for righteousness. By his wounds you have been healed. (1 Peter 2:24)

Sin damages us. Sin is like a deep cut, and we spend the rest of our lives bleeding out. Sin is like cancer, eating away at our soul and deteriorating our vital organs. Though our body breathes and lives on after the first sin, we are spiritually dead to God. Our name is not in the Book of Life because our destiny is hell. We earn that death like we earn the wages from our job.

However, God provides a gift for us. The gift of healing.

For the wages of sin is death, but the gift of God is eternal life in Christ Jesus our Lord. (Romans 6:23)

For you are saved by grace through faith, and this is not from yourselves; it is God's gift—not from works, so that no one can boast. (Ephesians 2:8–9)

If you earn your salvation, you get the credit. In that case, Jesus was just the negotiator who set up the deal that you finalized with your amazing attitude and good works.

No—salvation is a gift that you don't earn, but you receive.

"I give them eternal life, and they will never perish. No one will snatch them out of my hand." (John 10:28)

Nobody can snatch you out of Jesus' hand. Not your enemy. Not even Satan. But neither should you reject His gift of salvation, or take it for granted. As a priceless gift, it should always be treasured as an act of gratitude and worship to the One who saved you.

In Matthew 18:21–35, Jesus gives His disciples a sobering truth. He tells them the story of a servant who was forgiven of a huge debt that he owed to his master. Yet, after he was forgiven, he went out to a fellow servant who owed him a small amount and demanded full payment. When that servant could not pay, the wicked servant had him thrown in jail. When the master heard what the wicked servant had done, he called him back in and said. "After I mercifully forgave your debt, you refused to forgive someone else who only owed you a small amount? Well then, you too will be imprisoned until you have paid back your debt to me in full!"

Jesus told His disciples that God the Father would treat them the same way if they did not forgive their brothers and sisters from their heart. When God forgives you of your debt, then you should forgive others. That's truly following Christ.

Matthew 24:10–13 adds that in the final days, many will turn away from Jesus. But he that endures to the end will be saved.

That's why it is important to recognize that we need Him in our lives everyday, and to continue walking with Him everyday.

Salvation is a gift from God to those that believe. But when you receive it and truly believe, it WILL make a difference in your life. It's not based on your works, but your belief in Him. So believe and keep believing. He has a place for you in heaven when you do.

Now that we've taken care of your past. What about the future?

How should you now live knowing that you have salvation and a new identity in Jesus Christ?

SECTION 3

WHAT HAVE YOU BECOME?

CHAPTER 24

A NEW DAY

You hear the police sirens as you run into the house.

In the middle of the kitchen sits Mr. Ainsley, tied to a chair with Mr. Jenkins talking to the cops.

Realizing you're on the spot, you take it all in, quickly gather your words and announce, "Mr. Ainsley's innocent!"

A collective GASP fills the room.

"Officer, I realized I left my keys in chemistry class and Mr. Ainsley went out to the parking lot to find out whose car the keys belonged to. When he saw my tires were low, he drove the car down the street to his house to put air in them and discovered my brakes were bad. He then had the brake pads changed. Mr. Ainsley was trying to help me, not hurt me."

"Mr. Ainsley, is this true?"

"It is, Sir."

"Well, if that's the case, then I have no reason to take you in."

Ainsley drops his head and takes a big breath as you untie him. Mr. Jenkins looks disappointed but walks back to his golf cart.

Only you and Mr. Ainsley are left in the kitchen.

"Mr. Ainsley, I'm sorry this happened. Thank you for fixing my car."

"No problem. I'm just glad this is all over. Thank you for coming to my defense. I was trying to do the right thing."

You reach out your hand. Mr. Ainsley smiles and returns the gesture. You shake.

It's all over.

This story about the missing car and the chemistry teacher is a lighthearted way to look at a more serious subject of our sins in the eyes of God.

We're happy Mr. Ainsley was found not guilty and that his intentions were good.

But, in our case, we must realize our sins made us guilty. Nobody wins. Every hurt we imagined inflicting on someone else only hurt ourselves. Every sexual fantasy we imagined made us disgusting before God. Every curse word became offensive to God.

Sin made us vile, repugnant, and repulsive to God. Sin is so far from who God is—holy, righteous, perfect. He hates sin!

That's a small understanding of how God feels toward sin.

That's why it's so astounding that He sent His Son to die for us, then to declare those that believe in Him "not guilty."

You are forgiven.

FORGIVEN: to grant pardon for or remission of (an offense, debt, etc.); absolve; to cease to feel resentment against.[29]

You are justified.

JUSTIFIED: to show to be just or right; to declare innocent or guiltless; absolve; acquit.[30]

You are redeemed.

REDEEMED: to buy back; to recover by payment.[31]

God Himself, the one you offended, the one you despised, actually did all He could to release you from your punishment, buy you back from your slavery to sin, and make things right again.

What happens in your life now that you've been forgiven, justified, and redeemed?

RECIDIVISM: the tendency for a convicted criminal to return to jail; relapse.

There's a big, fancy vocabulary word for you. But here are some interesting stats on released prisoners who find themselves back in jail within nine years of being released.

- The 401,288 state prisoners released in 2005 had 1,994,000 arrests during the next nine-year period, an average of five arrests per released prisoner.

- An estimated 68 percent of released prisoners were arrested within three years, 79 percent within six years, and 83 percent within nine years.[32]

Why would someone experience prison then go out and do another crime, which could land them right back in prison?

There's lots of possible answers.

- Crime is a habit they can't break.
- Prison is a familiar place.
- Prison takes care of all their basic needs.
- Their friends are in prison.

So why would someone released from sin, go back and sin again?

- Habit
- It's familiar.
- They feel it takes care of their needs.
- Their friends are all doing it.

When someone gets released from prison they are given a second chance, a fresh start, a new opportunity to do better in their life. Why go back to the way they used to be?

Jesus stepped in and protected a woman caught in sexual sin from being stoned to death. When the accusers left:

Jesus straightened up and asked her, "Woman, where are they? Has no one condemned you?"

"No one, sir," she said.

"Then neither do I condemn you," Jesus declared. "Go now and leave your life of sin." (John 8:10–11 NIV)

Jesus told the woman not to return to the lifestyle she once knew. Now forgiven, she must find a new identity.

You too have a new identity in God's eyes.

Here's what the Bible has revealed so far about your identity:

1. **Who are you?** You were created by God who loves you.
2. **What have you done?** You are a sinner, but God saved you through Jesus Christ.

If you have believed in Jesus Christ, the Son of God, and received His forgiveness, the doors of the Prison of Sin have swung open and you step out a free man. He no longer sees you as a sinner or an enemy. God now sees you as a friend, righteous, clean, spotless, brand new, just like God the Father sees Jesus the Son.

We have to see ourselves that way—the way God sees us—so that we can stop doing the things that get us in trouble.

The Holy Spirit's fingerprints are all over our life. We have new rules to live by.

It's time to look at what you have become to fully understand your new Christ-shaped identity.

CHAPTER 25

A NEW LIFE

Go ask your mom if she would give birth to you all over again, but this time at your current size.

Is that a weird question to ask? Well someone asked Jesus that question.

In the Gospel of John, Jesus met with a Pharisee. A Pharisee was a super-religious rule-follower. Pharisees loved rules so much, they made up more of their own, in addition to all the commandments in the Bible. They added 613 more rules they felt made you more righteous, more "right" with God.[33]

Six hundred and thirteen!

So this Pharisee wanted to know how to live like Jesus. He wanted more rules to follow. It went like this:

There was a man from the Pharisees named Nicodemus, a ruler of the Jews. This man came to him at night and said, "Rabbi, we know that you are a teacher who has come from God, for no one could perform these signs you do unless God were with him."

Jesus replied, "Truly I tell you, unless someone is born again, he cannot see the kingdom of God."

"How can anyone be born when he is old?" Nicodemus asked him. "Can he enter his mother's womb a second time and be born?"

Jesus answered, "Truly I tell you, unless someone is born of water and the Spirit, he cannot enter the kingdom of God. Whatever is born of the flesh is flesh, and whatever is born of the Spirit is spirit. Do not be amazed that I told you that you must be born again. The wind blows where it pleases, and you hear its sound, but you don't know where it comes from or where it is going. So it is with everyone born of the Spirit."

"How can these things be?" asked Nicodemus. (John 3:1–9)

Jesus told Nicodemus that to live the Christian life you have to be born again. The Pharisee replied, "You mean, my mom has to give birth to me again?"

Jesus said, "No, that's flesh giving birth to flesh. I'm talking about Spirit giving birth to spirit."

You can't blame Nicodemus for responding this way. Jesus used the exact words one would use to mean being born a second time. However, His choice of words indicated that this birth was from a higher, better place.

Let's go back to the beginning. Genesis 2. God took the dirt, molded it into a man and breathed life into it. Adam was born.

Then, a short time later, Genesis 3, Adam and Eve sinned, and they were declared dead in their sins. Life was removed from them, even though they were still alive and breathing. What changed?

The Spirit was gone from them.

So now, in order to come back to life—true life, eternal life—God has to put that Spirit back into them. When someone accepts Jesus' death on the cross as a substitute for their own payment of death for their sins, that person comes spiritually alive.

The Spirit enters them. They have new life. They are born again.

When His Spirit is alive in you, you will not spiritually die.

Spirit = Life. No Spirit = Death.

Now that you have purified yourselves by obeying the truth so that you have sincere love for each other, love one another deeply, from the heart. For you have been born again, not of perishable seed, but of imperishable, through the living and enduring word of God. (1 Peter 1:22–23 NIV)

Newborns live by a different set of rules. Newborns don't hate, judge, or disassociate with people. They are dependent, and they love. Sure, they're fussy and messy, but the Father still loves them.

Now that you have a second chance in life, a new birth, obey the truth and love others deeply. God's love is in your heart.

CHAPTER 26

A NEW PERSPECTIVE

As of 2019, the tallest building in the world is in Dubai. It's called the Burj Khalifa, which means Building (Burg) of the King of the United Emirates (last name Khalifa). It stands 2,717 feet tall, 700 feet taller than the next tallest building, Shanghai Tower in China.[34]

The "King Building" gives you a different perspective of the world than you can get anywhere else.

Another tall building in America is the Willis Tower (formerly Sears Tower) standing at 1,450 feet and 110 stories in all. It has a glass bottom deck called the Skydeck that you can walk out on and step over the edge of the building.[35]

Cool or what?

Other tall buildings have this kind of observation deck—Petronas Twin Towers in Kuala Lumpur, Malaysia; Lotte World Tower in Seoul, South Korea; Shanghai World Financial Center in China; CN Tower in Toronto, Canada.

When you walk out and look down, everything seems so small. People look like ants, and cars look like small toys. However, if you stood on the ground and looked at those same people and cars, they would seem normal in size. Both perspectives are real, but both see things differently.

If you were stuck in traffic on the Pennsylvania Turnpike, it feels like you will be there forever. However, if you got in a helicopter you could see that the traffic clears up 500 yards ahead, just around the corner. Two perspectives on the same matter, with two different reactions.

How does God see things? From every perspective simultaneously and even perspectives we cannot understand.

Up close, God has compassion for the driver stuck in traffic. From up high, God sees hope. You, the driver, need to decide whether you will trust your perspective or trust God's perspective and be patient.

When you become a follower of Christ, your perspective changes. You see things from a different point of view. Not just from the ground level with all the dirt and grime, but also the top floor with the clouds and pure air.

READ THESE VERSES AND UNDERLINE WHAT NEW PERSPECTIVES ARE SEEN.

From now on, then, we do not know anyone from a worldly perspective. Even if we have known Christ from a worldly perspective, yet now we no longer know him in this way. Therefore, if anyone is in Christ, he is a new creation; the old has passed away, and see, the new has come! Everything is from God, who has reconciled us to himself through Christ and has given us the ministry of reconciliation. That is, in Christ, God was reconciling the world to himself, not counting their trespasses against them, and he has committed the message of reconciliation to us. (2 Corinthians 5:16–19)

Your new self can now see things above the worldly perspective mentioned in 2 Corinthians 5. Therefore, the passage says, since you are "in Christ," meaning you can learn to see things like He sees things, you are a new creation.

With our new perspective, we see Christ in a new way, not like the world sees Him. The world sees Him as ancient, outdated, and irrelevant. Now we see Him as intimate, loving, caring, and very present. The world thinks it was developed by random chance and evolution, but now we see that everything is from God. The world sees religion as rules and no fun. Now we see that Christ is about reconciliation and joy.

The old point of view you need to discard and replace. It was too limited and saw things with a narrow mind. You must upgrade with a wider field of vision, seeing things from an eternal perspective.

READ THIS PASSAGE IN EPHESIANS 4:17–32 AND UNDERLINE THE EVIDENCE OF SEEING THINGS A NEW WAY.

Therefore, I say this and testify in the Lord: You should no longer live as the Gentiles live, in the futility of their thoughts. They are darkened in their understanding, excluded from the life of God, because of the ignorance that is in them and because of the hardness of their hearts. They became callous and gave themselves over to promiscuity for the practice of every kind of impurity with a desire for more and more.

But that is not how you came to know Christ, assuming you heard about him and were taught by him, as the truth is in Jesus, to take off your former way of life, the old self that is corrupted by deceitful desires, to be renewed in the spirit of your minds, and to put on the new self, the one created according to God's likeness in righteousness and purity of the truth.

Therefore, putting away lying, speak the truth, each one to his neighbor, because we are members of one another. Be angry and do not sin. Don't let the sun go down on your anger, and don't give the devil an opportunity. Let the thief no longer steal. Instead, he is to do honest work with his own hands, so that he has something to share with anyone in need. No foul language should come from your mouth, but only what is good for building up someone in need, so that it gives grace to those who hear. And don't grieve God's Holy Spirit. You were sealed by him for the day of redemption. Let all bitterness, anger and wrath, shouting and slander be removed from you, along with all malice. And be kind and compassionate to one another, forgiving one another, just as God also forgave you in Christ.

This new perspective is amazing! Look at all it can see that you couldn't see before because you had an old self. So many features. So many positive qualities.

But wait, why doesn't it work like that all the time? Because you haven't changed your perspective. You now have permission to go to the top floor and yet you choose to stay on the ground. You can see things from God's view, but you've grown comfortable with your view.

> *So if you have been raised with Christ, seek the things above, where Christ is, seated at the right hand of God. Set your minds on things above, not on earthly things. For you died, and your life is hidden with Christ in God. When Christ, who is your life, appears, then you also will appear with him in glory. (Colossians 3:1–4)*

Step one—SEEK. Since your life has been raised to life by Jesus Christ, then seek out the things above, not the things below. Actively search for where Christ is working.

Step two—SET. Once you seek and find, then set your thoughts. Make it your home page. Put stakes in the ground and make it base camp. Remember, one day you will physically die and go be with Christ in heaven. It's the best view of eternity you'll ever find!

Step three—SLAUGHTER. Put to death those old sinful ways that came with that old sinful view of things.

> *Therefore, put to death what belongs to your earthly nature: sexual immorality, impurity, lust, evil desire,*

and greed, which is idolatry. Because of these, God's wrath is coming upon the disobedient, and you once walked in these things when you were living in them. But now, put away all the following: anger, wrath, malice, slander, and filthy language from your mouth. Do not lie to one another, since you have put off the old self with its practices and have put on the new self. You are being renewed in knowledge according to the image of your Creator. (Colossians 3:5–10)

LIST ALL THE THINGS IN COLOSSIANS 3:5–10 YOU NEED TO STOP DOING.

_____

_____

_____

You are in a new body, a new building with a new top floor perspective of the world. But you have to CHOOSE to go there. It wasn't there before. You had a sinful perspective until now.

Colossians says PUT IT TO DEATH and PUT IT AWAY. That's a choice. You have a new perspective. Go use it and then see the depth, width, and height of possibilities!

What can you see from God's perspective? Eternity.

CHAPTER 27

A NEW FAMILY

Family.

That word sparks a million different emotions in people.

For some—joy, comfort, love, unity

For others—pain, rejection, loss

Few words can ignite as much varying emotion as the word *family*.

If I were to say "ice cream," most would react in a similar fashion.

But "family" sets off the highest of highs and the lowest of lows in people. Some grew up in functional homes, where they genuinely loved and cared for one another. Others grew up in homes that could only be called disaster zones, where hate, selfishness, and ridicule ruled and everybody walked away damaged.

While an entire other book could be written about that (and many have been), we want to look at your new identity in Christ revealed to you through God's Word, and that includes getting a new family. Well, you don't throw out your old family, but your primary identity is now with a new family.

You have a new Father, a new brother, and a whole bunch of other brothers and sisters.

Jesus showed up and began talking about God in a new, familiar way. He didn't address God in the accepted titles used by Jews of the day that addressed His power, position, and abilities. Jesus called Him simply, "Father."

LIST ALL THE QUALITIES OF AN IDEAL FATHER.

_____

_____

_____

GO BACK AND CIRCLE THE QUALITIES THAT APPLY TO GOD.

While we need to respect our father on Earth, we aren't supposed to fear him in a "Oh no, he's home!" kind of way. Respect and honor must go hand-in-hand with love and devotion.

It's the same for our heavenly Father.

Every father gets that title because they have children. We are now to see God as our Father, who created us, molded us, provided for us, and gave us our identity. You have your earthly father's last name (or in some cases your mother's last name or your adopted parents' last name). That is your identity here on Earth.

Few people have the last name Hitler anymore. People dropped the name because they didn't want to be associated with Adolf whether they were related to him or not. If your last name is Samson, everyone thinks you're strong. Names create identity.

> *"For whoever does the will of my Father in heaven is my brother and sister and mother." (Matthew 12:50)*

If you desire God to be your spiritual Father, then Jesus is your brother.

Jesus was the first born of His family. He had earthly brothers and sisters born of Joseph and Mary. Jesus was born in Bethlehem, but He grew up in Nazareth. At thirty years old, Jesus returned to His hometown when word spread about Him, His miracles, and His claims to be God.

> *When Jesus had finished these parables, he left there. He went to his hometown and began to teach them in their synagogue, so that they were astonished and said, "Where did this man get this wisdom and these miraculous powers? Isn't this the carpenter's son? Isn't his mother called Mary, and his brothers James, Joseph, Simon, and Judas? And his sisters, aren't they all with us? So where does he get all these things?" And they were offended by him. (Matthew 13:53–57)*

> *Jesus entered a house, and the crowd gathered again so that they were not even able to eat. When his family heard this, they set out to restrain him, because they said, "He's out of his mind." (Mark 3:20–21)*

Wouldn't you? Sure, if He claimed He was God, you'd wonder. But later, when His family came to see Him, Jesus said this.

A crowd was sitting around him and told him, "Look, your mother, your brothers, and your sisters are outside asking for you."

He replied to them, "Who are my mother and my brothers?" Looking at those sitting in a circle around him, he said, "Here are my mother and my brothers! Whoever does the will of God is my brother and sister and mother." (Mark 3:32–35)

Did Jesus suddenly turn on His family and say, "Well if they think I'm crazy then I'm making you my family?" No, He wanted to make a point.

Blood makes us a part of an earthly family, but spirit makes us a part of a spiritual family.

Every time you go to church, it's a family reunion. Every time you eat with other believers, it's a family dinner. Your primary identity is with God's family while you love and respect your earthly family, no matter what they call you.

Some, when they become Christians, are ridiculed by their earthly family for believing in God. What do you do?

Respect your earthly father, but follow your spiritual Father.

Love your earthly brothers and sisters, but connect with your spiritual brothers and sisters.

For the one who sanctifies and those who are sanctified all have one Father. That is why Jesus is not ashamed to call them brothers and sisters, saying: I will proclaim your name to my brothers and sisters; I will sing hymns to you in the congregation. (Hebrews 2:11–12)

All believers have one Father, the same one Jesus calls Father. That makes Him our brother. The book of Hebrews says that Jesus "is not ashamed to call" you His brother.

There are probably times you are ashamed to tell others that the weird kid on the bus telling dumb jokes is your brother or the little girl running around singing is your sister.

But Jesus, despite all your mess-ups and embarrassing behavior (sin), feels perfectly fine saying, "Hey, he's my brother."

That's the way God wanted it to be. He wanted us to identify with His family.

For those he foreknew he also predestined to be conformed to the image of his Son, so that he would be the firstborn among many brothers and sisters. (Romans 8:29)

Jesus was the firstborn of this new family and you are a part of it. God wanted you to be like Jesus, the firstborn of this family.

The Gospels (Matthew, Mark, Luke, and John) tell the story of Jesus' birth, life, death, and resurrection, but the book of Acts details the formation of the church.

The writers used new terminology when addressing other believers.

Brothers and sisters is used over one hundred times in the New Testament to describe everyone who believes.

So now, not only is Jesus your brother, but all believers are now your brothers and sisters. You have millions of brothers and sisters who all call Jesus their brother and God their Father.

> *"In my Father's house are many rooms; if not, I would have told you. I am going away to prepare a place for you." (John 14:2)*

Jesus is in heaven preparing a place for you in your Father's house. This multi-room mansion will be shared by all believers. Your eternal home.

Imagine living for eternity with people you connect with, who love you, who respect you, who you get to know over time, who identify with you all because Jesus chose to identity with us. Where we'll worship God as one, talk and laugh and enjoy eating together as one big, joyful family.

We are family . . . forever.

CHAPTER 28

A NEW SPIRIT

WHEN YOU HAVE GUESTS COMING OVER, WHAT HAS TO HAPPEN TO GET THE HOUSE READY?

_____

_____

IF GOD SAID HE WAS COMING OVER TO YOUR HOUSE, WHAT WOULD YOU DO TO GET YOURSELF READY?

_____

_____

When you become a Christian, the biggest change to your identity is your spirit.

The Holy Spirit moves into you!

It's not a hostile takeover. It's willingly surrendering yourself to God and saying, "I'm all yours! Here are the keys. Come into my life!"

What does that mean to be filled with the Spirit and how can it change your life?

Before His crucifixion, Jesus promised His followers that His departure from Earth would be a good thing. In John 14, Jesus told them He would send them help when He left.

"If you love me, you will keep my commands. And I will ask the Father, and he will give you another Counselor to be with you forever. He is the Spirit of truth. The world is unable to receive him because it doesn't see him or know him. But you do know him, because he remains with you and will be in you." (John 14:15–17)

This Spirit, according to Jesus, would counsel us, give us direction, comfort, and advice. He would tell us the truth and be totally opposed to what the world would tell us to do. The world would not understand the Spirit's truth. Jesus went on.

"I have spoken these things to you while I remain with you. But the Counselor, the Holy Spirit, whom the Father will send in my name, will teach you all things and remind you of everything I have told you." (John 14:25–26)

The Holy Spirit would be our teacher and remind us of everything Jesus said.

Now, here's why Jesus' death was a good thing.

"Nevertheless, I am telling you the truth. It is for your benefit that I go away, because if I don't go away the

Counselor will not come to you. If I go, I will send him to you. When he comes, he will convict the world about sin, righteousness, and judgment: About sin, because they do not believe in me; about righteousness, because I am going to the Father and you will no longer see me; and about judgment, because the ruler of this world has been judged." (John 16:7–11)

Jesus had to leave so the Holy Spirit could move in. It was the final chapter of God's presence on Earth.

In the Old Testament, God created the earth and wanted to live with mankind. But mankind disobeyed God and brought sin into the picture. This is when everything changed. Yet, God still desired to have a relationship with man.

God then created a nation called Israel where He would show the world His power and use the nation as His platform for the unbelievable. After delivering them from slavery in Egypt and giving them the land He promised them (a.k.a. The Promised Land), a king arose named David who helped his son Solomon build a temple in Jerusalem. That temple became God's home on Earth. God lived (but was not confined to) a room called the Holy of Holies that used a thick curtain as a door.

A high priest entered that holy place once a year and encountered the presence of God's Spirit. It was so powerful, he could literally die if he walked in unprepared.

One thousand years after Solomon, Jesus arrived on Earth. Jesus, who is God's Son in human form, now walked around with mankind. When Jesus died on the cross, a powerful thing happened.

Then the curtain of the temple was torn in two from top to bottom. (Mark 15:38)

The barrier to the Holy of Holies was removed, revealing that man no longer had to go through a High Priest to get right with God. That old way of worshiping God had ended. A new "WAY" began. God's Spirit could now dwell in the heart of anyone who believed in His Son.

Three days after His death, Jesus rose from the dead! He walked around for forty days, proving His power and promise, then, as He departed, He said to His followers, "I will be with you always" as He ascended into heaven. How is that? How would Jesus be with us if He just ascended into heaven?

Around a week later, the Jews celebrated a holy-day called Pentecost, a day when the Jews thanked God for the harvest. But on that day, a different kind of harvest would occur.

When the day of Pentecost had arrived, they were all together in one place. Suddenly a sound like that of a violent rushing wind came from heaven, and it filled the whole house where they were staying. They saw tongues like flames of fire that separated and rested on each one of them. Then they were all filled with the Holy Spirit and began to speak in different tongues, as the Spirit enabled them. (Acts 2:1–4)

Now the Holy Spirit moved into the believers, filling them. God made His home in people.

Instead of being in one place (Jerusalem) or in one person (Jesus), the Holy Spirit moved into all believers, multiplying His effectiveness all over the world. He wants to be fruitful not just in one country or through one person, but through millions of individuals in every city and every country.

The Holy Spirit multiplies His effectiveness by multiplying His home in believers. So who is the Holy Spirit?

- He's God, the third person of the trinity. A "He" not an "it."
- He's equal to God and eternal like God because He IS God.
- He motivates believers with feelings, thoughts, decisions, ideas.

Think about it. If you are a believer . . . GOD LIVES INSIDE YOU! Not just for the weekend or a week, but for the rest of your life.

Your old spirit was dead, lifeless, empty, abandoned. That uninhabitable space was available. Now that you accepted Christ and made yourself a holy space, God moved in and set up shop and is ready to get to work.

And if God lives inside you, then on the day of your death, He will return to heaven, taking you with Him.

In him you also were sealed with the promised Holy Spirit when you heard the word of truth, the gospel of your salvation, and when you believed. The Holy Spirit is the down payment of our inheritance, until the redemption of the possession, to the praise of his glory. (Ephesians 1:13–14)

Now you have this NEW SPIRIT, the Holy Spirit, living inside you. So where are you two going to go together during your time on Earth?

To church? He loves worshiping God and fellowship with other believers.

To dinner with the family? That's good too.

How about to school? Yes, there's a lot you need to learn.

How about to the computer to watch porn? Wait, WHAT?

However, the body is not for sexual immorality but for the Lord, and the Lord for the body. God raised up the Lord and will also raise us up by his power. Don't you know that your bodies are a part of Christ's body? So should I take a part of Christ's body and make it part of a prostitute? Absolutely not! Don't you know that anyone joined to a prostitute is one body with her? For Scripture says, The two will become one flesh.

But anyone joined to the Lord is one spirit with him. (1 Corinthians 6:13–17)

If you join in on some sexual immorality, the Holy Spirit is right there inside you. Would you drag God into a strip club? No way! But if you go, God's right there too, inside you.

Flee sexual immorality! Every other sin a person commits is outside the body, but the person who is sexually immoral sins against his own body. Don't you know that your body is a temple of the Holy Spirit who is in you, whom you have from God? You are not your own, for you were bought at a price. So glorify God with your body. (1 Corinthians 6:18–20)

Don't turn your temple into a prostitute's bedroom.

That new life is an awesome thing. Don't abuse it. Fix it up. Pick up the garbage in your mind. Get things lined up.

Think of it, you are now the temple where God lives. God chose to live inside you so others can experience Him.

You are open for business wherever you go.

When you go to church, you take God there.

When you go to school, you take God there.

When you come home, you take God there.

God is there IN you.

Don't go where you shouldn't go. Don't do things that God would never do. You have the strength to be like Christ because the Spirit of God is right inside you.

You have power like you never had before, like the rushing wind felt on the day of Pentecost.

You can love like you've never loved before, like a passionate tongue of fire surrounding you.

You can make the best decisions you've ever made in your life.

It was a good thing that Jesus left Earth so the Holy Spirit could move in and spread Himself everywhere.

But we look forward to that family reunion when we'll meet up with the whole Trinity forever.

CHAPTER 29

A NEW MIND

In the movie *The Wizard of Oz*, a little girl and her dog get sucked up into a tornado and land in a Technicolor fantasy-land with height-challenged people and a green-skinned witch. Along the way, the girl meets a Scarecrow, a Tin Man, and a Cowardly Lion. They want to see the Wizard who rules the land and ask him for a few things—a brain, a heart, and courage.

Those are pretty good requests. We could all use those.

They meet the Wizard and he gives them what they want (sort of)—a diploma for brains, a ticking heart-shaped clock necklace for a heart, and a medal of honor for courage.

These days you can download a diploma online, buy a heart-shaped clock on Amazon, and bid on a medal on eBay.

Does that make you smart, loving, or courageous?

Hardly.

Some of the most foolish people in the world have brains and a PhD after their name. Some of the cruelest people have ticking hearts. And there are many cowards who wear badges on their uniforms.

Brains, heart, and courage come from within, and they are shaped by your identity.

And your identity is shaped by your mind. To have a mind like Christ, you must learn to think like He does.

For who has known the Lord's mind, that he may instruct him? But we have the mind of Christ. (1 Corinthians 2:16)

You're not going to be as smart as God, but you can have a mind that's wise, compassionate, and confident. When you were born, you received a self-loving, foolish mind. Over time it was shaped by the world—its messages and its temptations.

Then you became a Christian and a brand new you emerged. However, your mind is in need of righteous thinking. That takes practice, maturity, and time.

How does transformation happen in a Christian's life? Not overnight. It takes work, and a constant attention to what goes in and what comes out of your mind. As a Christian, the Holy Spirit who lives inside you gives you the wisdom and the tools to shape your mind.

The Wizard gave our friends little tokens to make them think that they were intelligent, kind, and brave. The Scarecrow, Tin Man, and Lion changed their thinking. They reset their minds with tools the Wizard gave them. Although this is just an analogy, there is a noteworthy aspect to this story. The characters learned to think differently.

It starts with FOCUS. We looked at this verse before, but we need to examine it again.

So if you have been raised with Christ, seek the things above, where Christ is, seated at the right hand of God. **Set your minds on things above, not on earthly things.** *For you died, and your life is hidden with Christ in God. When Christ, who is your life, appears, then you also will appear with him in glory. (Colossians 3:1–4)*

The Bible tells us to reset our thinking by changing our focus. On a camera, focus is crucial. Whatever is in focus in the image will draw the attention of everyone who sees it. But a good photographer knows that perspective changes the message of the photo as well. If you took a picture of a person while you stood on a chair, that person looks small and weak. If you took a picture of a person looking up while you laid on the ground at their feet, they look large and powerful.

Our mind must shift perspective and always look up to God, while focusing on Him and letting everything else just be blurry in the background. When we seek God's wisdom, it leads to greater understanding, compassion, and courage.

We must shift the way we think daily as we give ourselves constantly to God.

Therefore, brothers and sisters, in view of the mercies of God, I urge you to present your bodies as a living sacrifice, holy and pleasing to God; this is your true worship. Do not be conformed to this age, but be transformed by the renewing of your mind, so that you may discern

*what is the good, pleasing, and perfect will of God.
(Romans 12:1–2)*

Worship and sacrifice shift our focus and perspective and help in the transformation process as we feed our mind new thoughts.

This is a great time to mention that famous saying you may have heard from your parents: Garbage in . . . garbage out.

It means that if we put garbage into our minds, then our minds will process garbage, and fire garbage out of our mouths. It comes down to what you look at, think about, and consume on a daily basis.

WHERE ARE SOME PLACES WHERE YOU'VE PICKED UP SOME GARBAGE?

_____

_____

People are obsessed with their phones, iPads, and TV screens; shoveling stuff into their minds that slowly shifts how they think. Constantly watching horror movies will fill you with fear and violence. Constantly watching porn will fill your mind with lust.

Just walking down the street can be a struggle for your mind as temptations and thoughts bombard you everywhere you go. What are you supposed to do?

Capture every thought. Examine those thoughts before they become full-blown action. Question the thoughts. Don't let any thought go beyond godly approval.

Thoughts change you. This Christian mind wants to think like Christ, but if you feed it the wrong things, it won't work like it's supposed to. The apostle Paul showed us how to capture these bad thoughts.

Now I Paul, myself, appeal to you by the meekness and gentleness of Christ—I who am humble among you in person but bold toward you when absent. I beg you that when I am present I will not need to be bold with the confidence by which I plan to challenge certain people who think we are behaving according to the flesh. For although we live in the flesh, we do not wage war according to the flesh, since the weapons of our warfare are not of the flesh, but are powerful through God for the demolition of strongholds. We demolish arguments and every proud thing that is raised up against the knowledge of God, and we take every thought captive to obey Christ. (2 Corinthians 10:1–5)

PAUL'S THREE-STEP PROCESS TO HAVE A MIND LIKE CHRIST

1. Desire to be gentle and humble like Christ, not violent or arrogant.

2. Know the difference between the flesh (the world) and the spirit (the kingdom of heaven). This helps to identify the good from the bad.

3. Capture every thought, process it, demolishing bad thoughts and keeping the good.

We think our minds are a conveyor belt of thoughts, just pouring beyond our control. Yes, thoughts are pouring in beyond our control.

You can pick your friends, choosing the ones who fill your mind with positive thoughts.

You can limit what you see on screens, turning them off or looking away.

Then you must process every thought as it stands at the doorway of your mind.

If it glorifies God, loves people, and honors Christ, let it in. Dwell on it. Consume it.

If it hates God, hates people, and talks about lust, greed, or selfish pleasure, kick it out. Don't even think about it.

Don't just let the world back up a truckload of thoughts and dump them into your mind. You control the input. Thoughts only get as far as you let them.

Once you are committed to changing your mind, capturing all these thoughts and only allowing in those that are stamped "Christ-approved," your new mind will change everything. You'll begin to see improvements over time. What are the characteristics of the mind of Christ?

The mind of Christ serves God.

Thanks be to God through Jesus Christ our Lord! So then, with my mind I myself am serving the law of God. (Romans 7:25)

The mind of Christ sees clearly.

In their case, the god of this age has blinded the minds of the unbelievers to keep them from seeing the light of the gospel of the glory of Christ, who is the image of God. (2 Corinthians 4:4)

The mind of Christ seeks unity.

So that you may glorify the God and Father of our Lord Jesus Christ with one mind and one voice. (Romans 15:6)

The mind of Christ is peaceful.

And the peace of God, which surpasses all understanding, will guard your hearts and minds in Christ Jesus. (Philippians 4:7)

The mind of Christ is hopeful.

Therefore, with your minds ready for action, be sober-minded and set your hope completely on the grace to be brought to you at the revelation of Jesus Christ. (1 Peter 1:13)

We have to want this change and go off and seek it no matter the cost. God wants to give us this new mind and new way of thinking and He will give you more wisdom, more love, and more courage than you could ever imagine.

CHAPTER 30

A NEW POWER

WHAT SUPERHERO POWER WOULD YOU WANT?

_____

_____

The Avengers are a team of superheroes that unite to fight a common enemy. They each have unique superpowers.

- Ironman—super suit, genius, unlimited funds
- Hulk—gigantic with super strength and durability
- Black Panther—speed, stamina, reflexes, endurance.
- Spider-Man—wall-crawling, strength, agility, and spidey senses
- Captain America—super agility, strength, speed, and endurance
- Black Widow—intelligence, skilled, and super fighting moves

They all attained superhero status in different ways; some through science, through practice, by accident, or by being very smart.

What if I told you that you have a power that far exceeds any Avenger? You wouldn't believe it. You can't fly. You don't have super weapons. You can't defeat an army surrounding you.

No, but people in the Bible have displayed that kind of incredible power.

Elijah flew in a chariot of fire.

As they continued walking and talking, a chariot of fire with horses of fire suddenly appeared and separated the two of them. Then Elijah went up into heaven in the whirlwind. (2 Kings 2:11)

David beat a giant using a stone.

David put his hand in the bag, took out a stone, slung it, and hit the Philistine on his forehead. The stone sank into his forehead, and he fell facedown to the ground. (1 Samuel 17:49)

Samson took out an army with a donkey jawbone.

Then Samson said: With the jawbone of a donkey I have piled them in heaps. With the jawbone of a donkey I have killed a thousand men. (Judges 15:16)

What made Elijah, David, and Samson so special that they got superpowers?

They weren't perfect. But they were the right person at the right time, and God used them to accomplish His purpose. So if you're in the right place at the right time, who knows, maybe you could disappear like Philip the apostle . . .

When they came up out of the water, the Spirit of the Lord carried Philip away, and the eunuch did not see him any longer but went on his way rejoicing. (Acts 8:39)

Or heal people like Peter . . .

Then, taking him by the right hand he [Peter] raised him up, and at once his feet and ankles became strong. So he jumped up and started to walk, and he entered the temple with them—walking, leaping, and praising God. (Acts 3:7–8)

Or fight demons and heal the sick, like Paul.

God was performing extraordinary miracles by Paul's hands, so that even facecloths or aprons that had touched his skin were brought to the sick, and the diseases left them, and the evil spirits came out of them. (Acts 19:11–12)

You may do miraculous things in your lifetime, but you can't demand that you do miraculous things. Many who tried failed miserably.

Now some of the itinerant Jewish exorcists also attempted to pronounce the name of the Lord Jesus over those who had evil spirits, saying, "I command you by the Jesus that Paul preaches!" Seven sons of Sceva, a Jewish high priest, were doing this. The evil spirit answered them, "I know Jesus, and I recognize Paul—but who are you?" Then the man who had the evil spirit jumped on them, overpowered them all, and prevailed against them, so that they ran out of that house naked and wounded. (Acts 19:13–16)

That's embarrassing. To have the demons say to you, "Yeah, you're a nobody," then steal your clothes so you have to run away naked into the streets. Total humiliation. Don't try to overpower someone if you don't have the power.

You will receive that kind of power when God determines to give it to you. The real power you need is fighting the day-to-day battles of life. Those are the fears that defeat us.

Phobia comes from the Greek word *phobos,* which means fear or horror. They are anxiety disorders that affect 12.5 percent of American adults.[36]

Here are some phobias people deal with:

- acrophobia, fear of heights
- aerophobia, fear of flying
- arachnophobia, fear of spiders
- claustrophobia, fear of confined or crowded spaces
- ophidiophobia, fear of snakes
- zoophobia, fear of animals
- alektorophobia, fear of chickens
- onomatophobia, fear of names

- pogonophobia, fear of beards
- nephophobia, fear of clouds

Some of these you probably understand completely (spiders and snakes), while others you wonder, "what's so scary about a beard?" Then again, why is any Christian afraid of anything if they know Jesus?

For God has not given us a spirit of fear, but one of power, love, and sound judgment. (2 Timothy 1:7)

God doesn't want Christians running around scared of everything in life. We evangelize to the world through our confidence and faith.

What then are we to say about these things? If God is for us, who is against us? (Romans 8:31)

What enemy can destroy people who follow an all-powerful, indestructible God? Christians have eternal life. Knock a Christian down and they get back up on resurrection day.

Christians have the ability to fight temptation. Temptation takes out many heroes. Lust, drugs, and power are kryptonite. But God gives you the power to battle your weaknesses.

No temptation has come upon you except what is common to humanity. But God is faithful; he will not allow you to be tempted beyond what you are able, but with the temptation he will also provide a way out so that you may be able to bear it. (1 Corinthians 10:13)

Satan? He's been defeated and runs around trying to stay relevant. Here's your superpower against him:

Therefore, submit to God. Resist the devil, and he will flee from you. Draw near to God, and he will draw near to you. Cleanse your hands, sinners, and purify your hearts, you double-minded. (James 4:7–8)

Don't run like a coward. Run confidently to God.

In addition, you have a superhero suit. It's called the Full Armor of God.

Finally, be strengthened by the Lord and by his vast strength. Put on the full armor of God so that you can stand against the schemes of the devil. For our struggle is not against flesh and blood, but against the rulers, against the authorities, against the cosmic powers of this darkness, against evil, spiritual forces in the heavens. (Ephesians 6:10–12)

Your enemy is not flesh, and he can't bleed. He infiltrates the hearts and minds of people on Earth to do his dirty work. He's cosmic, evil, and spiritual. It's that devil again. Now that you know your enemy, you know how to defeat him. The "full armor" you need to put on comes in six pieces.

For this reason take up the full armor of God, so that you may be able to resist in the evil day, and having prepared everything, to take your stand. Stand, therefore, with truth like a belt around your waist, **righteousness** *like armor on your chest, and your feet sandaled with* **readiness** *for the gospel of peace. In every situation take up the shield of* **faith** *with which you can extinguish all the flaming arrows of the evil one. Take the helmet of* **salvation** *and the sword of the Spirit—which is the* **word of God***. (Ephesians 6:13–17)*

1. **Belt of truth**—Belts hold everything securely in place. Truth keeps it all together and gives you security.

2. **Breastplate of righteousness**—Being right with God protects your heart from discouragement and temptation.

3. **Shoes of readiness**—If you believe, then you're ready to go where called at a moment's notice. Warriors aren't lazy.

4. **Shield of faith**—Faith is hope, and faith is unseen. Your shield is unseen, and it protects the attacks that are unseen too. You trust it's there.

5. **Helmet of salvation**—Remind yourself that you are saved and nothing can separate you from the love of God.

6. **Sword of the Word**—The Word of God is a sharp, two-edged sword. It cuts through the lies and nonsense of this world.

WHICH PIECE OF ARMOR DO YOU NEED MORE OF RIGHT NOW?

_____

_____

_____

It takes spiritual armor to fight a spiritual enemy in your spiritual battles.

Also, if you love God, and God is on your side, then you have an army at your disposal.

> Then Micaiah said, "Therefore, hear the word of the LORD: I saw the LORD sitting on his throne, and the whole heavenly army was standing by him at his right hand and at his left hand." (1 Kings 22:19)

That army is unseen, but if you could see it all around you, you would never fear again.

> When the servant of the man of God got up early and went out, he discovered an army with horses and chariots surrounding the city. So he asked Elisha, "Oh, my master, what are we to do?"
>
> Elisha said, "Don't be afraid, for those who are with us outnumber those who are with them."
>
> Then Elisha prayed, "LORD, please open his eyes and let him see." So the LORD opened the servant's eyes, and

he saw that the mountain was covered with horses and chariots of fire all around Elisha. (2 Kings 6:15–17)

Your identity should no longer be associated with fear. God is on your side.

Above all, be strong and very courageous to observe carefully the whole instruction my servant Moses commanded you. Do not turn from it to the right or the left, so that you will have success wherever you go. (Joshua 1:7)

CHAPTER 31

A NEW SELF

Our computers and our phones get updates and upgrades all the time. Apps that we use come out with a new and improved version that we have to download to allow the program to run more smoothly and efficiently.

However, every time we get an upgrade, things change. Buttons are in a new place. The terminology changes. There are additional options you didn't have before that complicate the choices. It's better, yes, but it takes some getting used to.

Same thing for this new and improved identity—your new self. It too takes some time getting used to.

IF YOU COULD UPDATE YOURSELF, WHERE WOULD YOU START?

_____

_____

Would you start with your clothes or hairstyle?
The situation you're living in?
Your school? Your friends? Your family?
What about your inner "self"?

The word *self* in the Bible comes from the word *anthrōpos* which you probably recognize from the word *anthropology*.

Anthropology is the science and study of human beings, their origin, evidence, nature, and destiny.

Anthrōpos means human being. So, what does "new self" mean in the Bible?

It means you are a brand new human being. A new person. Your complete identity has changed. You now have new choices to make, especially when it comes to your daily behavior.

Before, you had no choice. You did what you did because your old self ruled your thinking.

The apostle Paul, one of the greatest names in the New Testament, used to drag Christians out of their homes, send them to court, and oversaw the stoning death of some he felt disobeyed his religion. He approved the death of one man, named Stephen, who did nothing wrong except worship Jesus.

Then Paul, on a road to the city of Damascus, met Jesus live and in person, and his life changed. Now he no longer wanted to destroy churches, but to start them in cities all over Asia.

Paul knew the dramatic difference between his old self and his new self. He struggled with his sinfulness. In Romans 6, Paul revealed this battle and you will probably identify with him.

What should we say then? Should we continue in sin so that grace may multiply? Absolutely not! How can we who died to sin still live in it? (Romans 6:1–2)

We can't keep sinning with the expectation that God will forgive us (even though He will if you are truly saved). We should want to stop sinning out of respect for God.

Or are you unaware that all of us who were baptized into Christ Jesus were baptized into his death? Therefore we were buried with him by baptism into death, in order that, just as Christ was raised from the dead by the glory of the Father, so we too may walk in newness of life. (Romans 6:3–4)

Baptism means to be "fully immersed." Paul compared a water baptism (fully immersed) to the Christian life (fully immersed). We are "all in" as Christians. Our old selves were buried in a grave (like Jesus) and our new selves came to life (like Jesus). Jesus went into the grave with His old body and emerged with a new resurrected body. We too have a new self.

For if we have been united with him in the likeness of his death, we will certainly also be in the likeness of his resurrection. For we know that our old self was crucified with him so that the body ruled by sin might be rendered powerless so that we may no longer be enslaved to sin, since a person who has died is freed from sin. (Romans 6:5–7)

If we claim to be united with Jesus, then we put to death the old behavior and live now with a new behavior. Jesus lived in a human body and chose to crucify it on the cross, putting it to death. We chose that same thing, putting our old selves to death, putting it on the cross, killing it, and rendering it powerless.

> *Now if we died with Christ, we believe that we will also live with him, because we know that Christ, having been raised from the dead, will not die again. Death no longer rules over him. For the death he died, he died to sin once for all time; but the life he lives, he lives to God. So, you too consider yourselves dead to sin and alive to God in Christ Jesus. (Romans 6:8–11)*

Now that we've put off that old self, we agree to live as a new self in Jesus. Jesus arose in a resurrected, indestructible body. That's us too! Jesus died once for all our sin. Now He lives for God and so should we. Sin is dead in our lives.

> *Therefore do not let sin reign in your mortal body, so that you obey its desires. And do not offer any parts of it to sin as weapons for unrighteousness. But as those who are alive from the dead, offer yourselves to God, and all the parts of yourselves to God as weapons for righteousness. For sin will not rule over you, because you are not under the law but under grace. (Romans 6:12–14)*

If sin is dead, why do we try to bring it back to life?

We have a choice—offer ourselves to GOD or offer ourselves to SIN.

But sin is powerful. At times, you probably make strong statements in your heart, like I'M NOT GOING TO SIN EVER AGAIN, then ten minutes later . . . sin.

Can you ever really defeat sin completely in your life? Yes and No.

YES—because Jesus defeated the power of sin to separate you from God forever.

NO—because we still live in sinful bodies in a sinful world. We continue to give sin control over our choices.

How do you fully activate this new sinless self and live by its full potential?

Once again, Paul understood the struggle and gave us a battle plan to defeat sin once and for all.

READ EPHESIANS 5:1–21 AND UNDERLINE WHAT YOU NEED TO DO TO NOT SIN.

Therefore, be imitators of God, as dearly loved children, and walk in love, as Christ also loved us and gave himself for us, a sacrificial and fragrant offering to God. But sexual immorality and any impurity or greed should not even be heard of among you, as is proper for saints. Obscene and foolish talking or crude joking are not suitable, but rather giving thanks. For know and recognize this: Every sexually immoral or impure or greedy person, who is an idolater, does not have an inheritance in the kingdom of Christ and of God.

Let no one deceive you with empty arguments, for God's wrath is coming on the disobedient because of these things. Therefore, do not become their partners. For you were once darkness, but now you are light in the Lord. Live as children of light—for the fruit of the light consists of all goodness, righteousness, and truth—testing what is pleasing to the Lord. Don't participate in the fruitless works of darkness, but instead expose them. For it is shameful even to mention what is done by them in secret. Everything exposed by the light is made visible, for what makes everything visible is light. Therefore it is said:

> *Get up, sleeper, and rise up from the dead,*
> *and Christ will shine on you.*

Pay careful attention, then, to how you live—not as unwise people but as wise—making the most of the time, because the days are evil. So don't be foolish, but understand what the Lord's will is. And don't get drunk with wine, which leads to reckless living, but be filled by the Spirit: speaking to one another in psalms, hymns, and spiritual songs, singing and making music with your heart to the Lord, giving thanks always for everything to God the Father in the name of our Lord Jesus Christ, submitting to one another in the fear of Christ.

Here's a list of all the sins YOU SHOULD NOT DO from Ephesians 5:1–21:

- Sexual immorality.
- Impurity.
- Greed.
- Obscene and foolish talking.
- Crude joking.
- Idolizing anything but God.
- Participation in fruitless works of darkness.
- Drunkenness.
- Reckless living.

Here's a list of all the things YOU SHOULD DO from Ephesians 5:1–21:

- Imitate God.
- Walk in love.
- Give thanks.
- Don't be deceived.
- Live as children of the light—goodness, righteousness, truth.
- Test whether something is pleasing to God.
- Expose darkness.
- Pay attention to how you live.
- Make the most of your time on Earth.
- Be filled by the Spirit.
- Speak encouragement and praise to others.
- Make music with your heart.
- Submit to one another.

There you have it. The list of do's and don'ts. Looks great on paper. But HOW can you activate those qualities in your life?

CHOOSE

Everything listed above is a choice.

Do I say something crude or encouraging?

Do I get drunk or not?

Do I think sexual thoughts about someone or imitate Christ?

Do I do the work of darkness or expose it as wrong?

Do I idolize the world or get filled with the Spirit?

It's a choice. Your old self says, "choose the world!" Your new self (the Spirit) whispers, "choose Jesus."

If you choose sin, you remain in the world.

If you choose Jesus, you remain in Him.

Where you remain will determine whether you are living as the old self or the new self.

> *Everyone who remains in him does not sin; everyone who sins has not seen him or known him.*
>
> *Children, let no one deceive you. The one who does what is right is righteous, just as he is righteous. The one who commits sin is of the devil, for the devil has sinned from the beginning. The Son of God was revealed for this purpose: to destroy the devil's works. Everyone who has been born of God does not sin, because his seed remains in him; he is not able to sin, because he has been*

born of God. This is how God's children and the devil's children become obvious. Whoever does not do what is right is not of God, especially the one who does not love his brother or sister. (1 John 3:6–10)

If you choose to remain in Christ, you won't sin.

If you listen to the devil's deception and choose to sin, you will sin.

But if you do sin, know that He will treat you as a son and discipline you. And remember this: you can choose whether to sin or not, but you do not get to choose the discipline He gives you. So why not just stay as close to Jesus as possible.

His favor is priceless.

CHAPTER 32

A NEW FINAL DESTINATION

DO YOU WANT TO KNOW YOUR FUTURE?

_____

_____

HOW FAR INTO THE FUTURE WOULD YOU WANT TO KNOW? A WEEK, A MONTH, A YEAR, TEN YEARS?

_____

_____

There was a time, not so long ago, when we thought that we would be flying around in space cars or rocketing to school with jetpacks strapped to our backs. We thought lasers would replace bullets, and robots would be our servants.

No kidding. In 1975, there was a show called *Space 1999*, about the colonization of the moon. While we've made some great strides in technology, the future isn't as "futuristic" as we thought.

We're not very good at accurately predicting our future. Some people want to know their future, so they go to palm readers and astrologers thinking they will get a sneak peek to know what to expect. These prophets are fakes and have no idea what the future holds. Only God knows.

What if God told you that you would die in six months, twelve days, and seven hours? Would it motivate you or terrify you? Would you live purposefully or recklessly?

It could be scary to know your future or it could be a relief.

You probably have a lot of the same questions as other guys your age:

- Will I do well in school?
- Will I graduate?
- Where will I go to college?
- Who will I marry?
- What kind of career will I have?
- Will I be rich or poor?
- Will I be healthy?
- When will I die?

How does God answer those questions?

"Trust me. You're on a need-to-know basis." God will tell you when you need to know.

It's called faith. We must trust that God knows what's best for us.

In the book of Jeremiah, God wrote this to the nation of Israel, His nation, the one He created:

"For I know the plans I have for you"—this is the LORD's declaration—"plans for your well-being, not for disaster, to give you a future and a hope. You will call to me and come and pray to me, and I will listen to you. You will seek me and find me when you search for me with all your heart. I will be found by you"—this is the LORD's declaration—"and I will restore your fortunes and gather you from all the nations and places where I banished you"—this is the LORD's declaration. "I will restore you to the place from which I deported you." (Jeremiah 29:11–14)

The people were about to be punished for seventy years because of their sins, but God still reassured them saying, "The present is going to be tough, but I have great things planned for you in the future."

Does that sentiment apply to you or only to Israel? Why not you? God has wonderful plans for you—plans for your good, to give you hope. He wants to be side-by-side with you, talking to you as you listen to Him, seek Him, find Him. God wants to be found by you and restore the things you lost. He has a place for you.

He's not specific about those future plans, but He reveals to you a few clues that determine how you should live today, and how to shape your identity for the future.

If you believe in Jesus Christ and He has a relationship with you, here is your future. No crystal balls. No tarot cards. No palm reading. Just the Word of God.

First of all, you will receive eternal life.

"Truly I tell you, anyone who hears my word and believes him who sent me has eternal life and will not come under judgment but has passed from death to life." *(John 5:24)*

This is eternal life: that they may know you, the only true God, and the one you have sent—Jesus Christ. *(John 17:3)*

You will not ever be separated from the giver of life, but dwell with God as He always wanted His beloved creations to do.

You will be an heir.

Blessed be the God and Father of our Lord Jesus Christ. Because of his great mercy he has given us new birth into a living hope through the resurrection of Jesus Christ from the dead and into an inheritance that is imperishable, undefiled, and unfading, kept in heaven for you. You are being guarded by God's power through faith for a salvation that is ready to be revealed in the last time. *(1 Peter 1:3–5)*

An heir has an inheritance. When your parents die, you may receive something from their estate. When you die, you will receive something from God—kind of a reverse inheritance. It can't perish. It won't deteriorate. And it's stored safely in heaven. What is it? Eternal life, a room in your Father's house, abundant food, whatever you need to live forever . . .

You get to go to heaven.

If you read Revelation 21, it will give you a tour through your future home.

Here are some highlights:

- It's a new heaven and a new earth.
- There's a holy city called New Jerusalem.
- God will be there face-to-face with His people.
- There won't be any crying, sorrow, or pain.
- You'll see angels.
- Heaven is beautiful.
- Other people from all throughout history will be there.
- Jesus will be there.
- It never, ever ends. Not ever.

Whatever you do, do it from the heart, as something done for the Lord and not for people, knowing that you will receive the reward of an inheritance from the Lord. You serve the Lord Christ. (Colossians 3:23–24)

You will be receiving everything you need when you die, so how does that change your treatment of the stuff you have now? It is just stuff. It will break or fall apart or you will leave it behind because you can't take it with you.

In heaven, your heart will be fulfilled by the Lord.

He poured out his Spirit on us abundantly through Jesus Christ our Savior so that, having been justified by his grace, we may become heirs with the hope of eternal life. This saying is trustworthy. I want you to insist on these things, so that those who have believed God might be careful to devote themselves to good works. These are good and profitable for everyone. (Titus 3:6–8)

Before all this happens, there will be one more event in the future: JESUS' RETURN.

"I am," said Jesus, "and you will see the Son of Man seated at the right hand of Power and coming with the clouds of heaven." (Mark 14:62)

When He comes back, He's taking His followers with Him.

Do not be amazed at this, because a time is coming when all who are in the graves will hear his voice and come out. (John 5:28–29)

You will step out of your grave and be given a resurrected body, a fully restored version of you put into a never-deteriorating body.

Now that you know who you will be for eternity, that should change how you think about yourself today and tomorrow.

Jesus asked probably the most important question ever asked in the Bible.

Jesus said to her, "I am the resurrection and the life. The one who believes in me, even if he dies, will live. Everyone who lives and believes in me will never die. <u>Do you believe this</u>?" (John 11:25–26)

How you answer this question changes everything about your life:

DO YOU BELIEVE JESUS WILL RESURRECT THOSE WHO BELIEVE IN HIM?

_____

_____

DO YOU BELIEVE JESUS WILL GIVE ETERNAL LIFE TO ALL THOSE HE RESURRECTS?

_____

_____

DO YOU BELIEVE YOU WILL BE RESURRECTED WHEN YOU DIE AND LIVE ETERNALLY?

_____

_____

God reveals to you this truth to shape you into the image of Christ today.

CHAPTER 33

A NEW LOVE

WHAT DOES LOVE FEEL LIKE?

_____

_____

What is love? Poets, songwriters, romance authors have all explored love and they tend to say the same thing over and over.

1. **It's a feeling**—a guy in love says he feels tingly, important, and special.
2. **It's in one's mind**—a guy thinks about that girl all the time.

Those things are true, but then the world tends to go in the wrong direction regarding love.

The world thinks love is mainly physical, so it needs to be expressed with sex.

The world believes love needs physical action that the Bible says is only reserved for marriage. In marriage, love is expressed through sex after committing to one another and should not be something shared outside of marriage.

Don't believe me? The Bible clearly reveals that sentiment.

UNDERLINE ALL THE WORDS THAT DEAL WITH SEXUAL SIN

I am afraid that when I come again my God will humble me before you, and I will be grieved over many who have sinned earlier and have not repented of the impurity, sexual sin and debauchery in which they have indulged. (2 Corinthians 12:21 NIV)

But among you there must not be even a hint of sexual immorality, or of any kind of impurity, or of greed, because these are improper for God's holy people. (Ephesians 5:3 NIV)

The acts of the flesh are obvious: sexual immorality, impurity and debauchery. (Galatians 5:19 NIV)

That is why a man leaves his father and mother and is united to his wife, and they become one flesh. (Genesis 2:24 NIV)

Marriage should be honored by all, and the marriage bed kept pure, for God will judge the adulterer and all the sexually immoral. (Hebrews 13:4 NIV)

Or do you not know that wrongdoers will not inherit the kingdom of God? Do not be deceived: Neither the sexually immoral nor idolaters nor adulterers nor men who have sex with men. (1 Corinthians 6:9 NIV)

Flee from sexual immorality. All other sins a person commits are outside the body, but whoever sins sexually, sins against their own body. (1 Corinthians 6:18 NIV)

"But I tell you that anyone who looks at a woman lustfully has already committed adultery with her in his heart." (Matthew 5:28 NIV)

It is God's will that you should be sanctified: that you should avoid sexual immorality; that each of you should learn to control your own body in a way that is holy and honorable, not in passionate lust like the pagans, who do not know God. (1 Thessalonians 4:3–5 NIV)

Drink water from your own cistern, running water from your own well. Should your springs overflow in the streets, your streams of water in the public squares? Let them be yours alone, never to be shared with strangers. May your fountain be blessed, and may you rejoice in the wife of your youth. A loving doe, a graceful deer— may her breasts satisfy you always, may you ever be intoxicated with her love. (Proverbs 5:15–19 NIV)

There's also an entire book of the Bible called Song of Songs that is very detailed and graphic (using similes and metaphors) about sex between two married people.

So now that we know the parameters of sex and we don't confuse that with love, let's get back to our question—what is love?

It is the first fruit Paul expressed when listing the fruit of the Spirit,

> *But the fruit of the Spirit is love, joy, peace, patience, kindness, goodness, faithfulness, gentleness, and self-control. The law is not against such things. (Galatians 5:22–23)*

Jesus quoted an expression from the Old Testament that was used, in some way, ten times from the book of Deuteronomy. Ten is a lot, and Moses the writer emphasized it so much because he wanted it to sink in. Jesus brought that statement back to life by quoting it Himself and revealing to us what love is.

> *"Love the Lord your God with all your heart, with all your soul, with all your mind, and with all your strength." (Mark 12:30)*

Love is not just a feeling (heart) or just in one's head (mind) or simply expressed in one's body (strength) . . . it's all that and more.

It's a complete and total commitment of your entire self—your heart, your soul, your mind, and your body.

It's the same kind of love God has for you.

I pray that you, being rooted and firmly established in love, may be able to comprehend with all the saints what is the length and width, height and depth of God's love, and to know Christ's love that surpasses knowledge, so that you may be filled with all the fullness of God. (Ephesians 3:17–19)

You cannot fully comprehend how long, wide, high, and deep God's love is for you. It's as long, wide, high, and deep as He is, and He extends to infinity. This kind of love is ALL IN with everything God has.

And with that love for you, He can do just about anything with your life.

Now to him who is able to do above and beyond all that we ask or think according to the power that works in us—to him be glory in the church and in Christ Jesus to all generations, forever and ever. Amen. (Ephesians 3:20–21)

Love is power, more powerful than we can ever imagine. And if it can do all that, it requires all that we have.

These four areas define all of you:

HEART: the center of your emotions, feelings, passions

SOUL: your spirit, your personality or self, your inner person that lives forever

MIND: your thoughts, your intelligence, your creativity, reason, logic, organization

STRENGTH: your body, flesh, will power

You can't effectively love God with only one area. Two falls short. Three is better, but four is ideal. It leaves no room for error or allowing anything else to creep in and take over.

If you can root yourself in that kind of love for God and establish yourself firmly in His love, then you will be able to love others better than you ever imagined.

It begins with commitment.

First, you determine who to love. In this case—God. Why?

We love because he first loved us. (1 John 4:19)

You realize God loves you immeasurably more than you can ever imagine, so you respond by loving Him back that way.

Then, COMMIT ALL OF YOU to love God.

Love Him with all your emotions.

Love Him with all your thoughts.

Love Him with all your logic.

Love Him with all your personality.

Love Him with all your time.

Love Him with all your reason.

Love Him with all your creativity.

Love Him wherever you go.

Love God by obeying.

You want to show love to your parents? Obey them. Follow the rules. Listen to their advice. The fifth commandment says to honor your mother and father. You honor them by obeying them. Just ask them; they'll tell you.

Jesus gave the same definition of love when talking about relationship with God.

> *"I will not leave you as orphans; I am coming to you. In a little while the world will no longer see me, but you will see me. Because I live, you will live too. On that day you will know that I am in my Father, you are in me, and I am in you. The one who has my commands and keeps them is the one who loves me. And the one who loves me will be loved by my Father. I also will love him and will reveal myself to him."*
>
> *Judas (not Iscariot) said to him, "Lord, how is it you're going to reveal yourself to us and not to the world?"*
>
> *Jesus answered, "If anyone loves me, he will keep my word. My Father will love him, and we will come to him and make our home with him. The one who doesn't love me will not keep my words. The word that you hear is not mine but is from the Father who sent me." (John 14:18–24)*

Jesus said "the one who has my commands and keeps them" shows love to his Father and shows love to Him. Jesus promised to set up His home in the hearts of those who do what He asks.

So how do you obey God and show your love to Him?

First Corinthians 13:4–8 is all about love. If you do these things, you will show love to God and He will in turn reveal Himself to you.

- Be patient.
- Be kind.
- Don't envy.
- Don't boast or be proud.
- Don't dishonor others.
- Don't be self-seeking.
- Don't be easily angered.
- Keep no record of wrongs.
- Don't delight in evil but rejoice with the truth.
- Always protect.
- Always trust.
- Always hope.
- Always persevere.

You won't fail to love if you obey God first.

SECTION 4

WHERE ARE YOU GOING?

CHAPTER 34

WHAT'S NEXT?

Mr. Ainsley and you walk outside.

You want to say something to him, but struggle. The words don't come easily, not because you're not an articulate speaker, but because you know you have to show some humility.

"Mr. Ainsley, I'm sorry."

Mr. Ainsley stops walking and turns. He smiles in a way you haven't seen during this entire ridiculous accusation.

"It's okay. I knew it would all work out. I thought I could fix your car and get it back before you went looking for it. I should have just asked you beforehand. Still, I'm glad you had a chance to discover something about me. You see, I'm a Christian."

That surprises you. All the kids love him because he's always nice and respectful. That's why stealing cars seemed so unusual and out of character. Yet, fixing kids' cars is definitely Mr. Ainsley.

Yet, you find it interesting that he's both a scientist and a Christian.

"But you're a chemistry teacher. How do you balance science and faith"?

He laughs. "Science and faith are not against each other. Science is about looking at the evidence and finding the truth it points to. We build bridges between facts. Sometimes those bridges are solid and true, and sometimes those bridges are long shots and ill-supported. I believe science and faith support each other. Much of science relies on faith, just like Christianity. In both, we look at the clues that have been revealed and make decisions based on what we know."

"Where do you find evidence of God?"

Mr. Ainsley looked around. "Everywhere. Nature. In people. In my wife and daughter. In the Bible. It tells the history of God and Jesus Christ, but it also tells your history."

"My history?"

"Sure," Mr. Ainsley said. "If you're a person living on Earth, then the Bible reveals to you how to live and what your future will be. It describes your identity."

"My identity? But I know who I am."

Mr. Ainsley paused, "Who you are meant to be."

As an investigator this intrigued you. Mr. Ainsley suggested to you a book that could give you evidence about your true identity.

Now back to our investigation.

You've looked into the facts.

The truth has been revealed.

You discovered that you're a criminal (a sinner) and your crimes against the law (God) will send you away forever (hell). Your defense attorney (Jesus) told you to declare yourself guilty (confession) as you stood before the judge (the Father). The judge declared you guilty and sentenced you to prison (hell) for (eternal) life. However, good news, your defense attorney (Jesus) stood up and offered to take your entire punishment for you (redemption), allowing you to be set free for life (salvation).

It's a new day. You are born again.

You have a new self, family, spirit, mind, power, love, and . . . future.

What do you do now? Live life the way you've always lived it? Same ol', same ol'?

Remember what the prophet Jeremiah said.

> *"For I know the plans I have for you"—this is the LORD's declaration—"plans for your well-being, not for disaster, to give you a future and a hope." (Jeremiah 29:11)*

God has plans for you, a future and a hope. It's not just to wait for the future, but plans for this life.

He has a mission designed for you.

The book of Proverbs makes this clear.

> *To humans belong the plans of the heart,*
> *but from the LORD comes the proper answer of the tongue.*
> *All a person's ways seem pure to them,*
> *but motives are weighed by the LORD.*

Commit to the LORD whatever you do,
and he will establish your plans.
The LORD works out everything to its proper end—
even the wicked for a day of disaster.
(Proverbs 16:1–4 NIV)

In their hearts humans plan their course,
but the LORD establishes their steps. (Proverbs 16:9 NIV)

Many are the plans in a person's heart,
but it is the LORD's purpose that prevails.
(Proverbs 19:21 NIV)

There is no wisdom, no insight, no plan
that can succeed against the LORD. (Proverbs 21:30 NIV)

You don't have the power to work everything out to the end. God does. He can even determine the course of an evil person's life, someone who doesn't love Him. But if you love Him and commit to Him . . . wow . . . imagine what He can do with that.

Plus He knows you and He wants you to be fruitful. The eternal creator, God, wants to create a life path for you that'll fulfill you and bring Him glory.

How can you say no to that? Don't put off getting on the path God designed for your life. God has revealed it to you. Maybe not all the specifics, but the tools and characteristics you'll need to get you there.

God has plans and a purpose for you. He saved you for a reason. He wants you to be part of His work.

It's not time to relax. It's time to get busy. You've got work to do.

God has revealed Himself to you . . . now you must reveal Him to the world.

CHAPTER 35

DO GOOD WORKS

You're probably at the age (or will be soon) where you have a job, or are looking to get a job.

Work is a good thing. We were designed to work. When God made Adam in the garden, He gave him a job to do—take care of the garden. The first job in the Bible was a gardener. The second job God gave Adam was to name the animals. Adam looked at every animal and gave a name to each one as it passed by.

Throughout your life, you will have fun jobs and challenging jobs. Jobs that you can't wait to wake up and go to and jobs you hide from under your blankets. All jobs teach us something about our limitations, our strengths, and God's possibilities.

God saved you, remade you, and now has plans for you.

For we are his workmanship, created in Christ Jesus for good works, which God prepared ahead of time for us to do. (Ephesians 2:10)

Workmanship means the degree of craftsmanship put into something. It describes an artist, a handyman, an architect, a builder.

You were designed, carefully, not randomly. God had specific plans for you to do something. What is it?

Good works.

And He planned those good works for you long ago, way before you were made.

He said, "I know exactly what I'm going to do with _____ (INSERT NAME HERE). He's going to do some good things for me in his world."

What could keep God's plans of good works from happening in your life?

You.

You will say to me, therefore, "Why then does he still find fault? For who can resist his will?" But who are you, a mere man, to talk back to God? Will what is formed say to the one who formed it, "Why did you make me like this?" Or has the potter no right over the clay, to make from the same lump one piece of pottery for honor and another for dishonor? (Romans 9:19–21)

Imagine you're in art class and today's project is to make a cup out of clay. You begin to mold the clay into the shape of a cup. But the clay resists. It's as hard as a rock. No design is possible. No workmanship. It remains a big, useless clump of clay.

Then to make matters worse, the clay talks back to you.

Clay: *What are you doing?*

You: *I'm trying to make a cup out of you.*

Clay: Why?

You: Cups are very useful. They hold liquids that bring refreshment to people. They hold water so people can take their medicine for healing. They hold chemicals and protect people from harm.

Clay: I don't want to be a cup.

You: Oh? What do you want to be?

Clay: I want to be a beautiful statue in a museum, admired and loved by many who come by and take selfies with me in the background.

WHAT WOULD YOU DO WITH THIS LUMP OF CLAY THAT RESISTS YOUR PLANS FOR IT?

_____

_____

Trash. If the clay's not cooperating with you, then it's no use to you.

Are you that way with God? Resistant? Argumentative?

Become a malleable, bendable, flexible piece of clay in the hands of God.

God has many jobs for His new creations.

Now in a large house there are not only gold and silver vessels, but also those of wood and clay; some for honorable use and some for dishonorable. So if anyone purifies himself from anything dishonorable, he will be a special instrument, set apart, useful to the Master, prepared for every good work. (2 Timothy 2:20–21)

There are many different types of people in this world. Rich and poor. Skilled and unskilled. Thinkers and doers. Athletic and not athletic.

Whether you are gold or wood, silver or clay, you have a good work to do, but you must be willing to be used. God has something for you to do. It may get attention and awards, or it may be working behind the scenes.

What God asks you to do may get cheers from other students or trash talk behind your back. It doesn't matter. As long as you do it with a pure heart and pure intentions to please God and be obedient, you are doing what you are designed to do.

Obedience requires flexibility, no matter the cost.

Therefore, my dear friends, just as you have always obeyed, so now, not only in my presence but even more in my absence, work out your own salvation with fear and trembling. For it is God who is working in you both to will and to work according to his good purpose. (Philippians 2:12–13)

How do you "work out your salvation"?

You are not saved by works, but by your belief in Jesus Christ.

This means that you have salvation, now how are you going to exercise it?

How are you going to live, work, accomplish, achieve, bring results?[37]

And do it with a certain amount of fear—fearful that if you don't do what you've been designed to do you'll disappoint your heavenly Father, hurt others, and miss the opportunities you could achieve.

It's a very good purpose that God has for you.

Don't fight with God and get tossed in the recyclable clay pile.

You are God's workmanship created to do good works for God . . . so let's get after it!

CHAPTER 36

WORSHIP GOD

Your new-and-improved self can't help but love God. It has fallen in love with the God who loved you first and died for you completely, all before you knew Him and after you rejected Him. It's a beautiful love story.

Let's remember what we said about love so far.

Love the Lord your God with all your heart, with all your soul, with all your mind, and with all your strength. (Mark 12:30)

We know that to love God, you must do it with everything you have—all your heart, all your soul, all your mind, and all your strength. It's a full commitment.

Jesus answered, "If anyone loves me, he will keep my word. My Father will love him, and we will come to him and make our home with him. The one who doesn't love me will not keep my words. The word that you hear is not mine but is from the Father who sent me." (John 14:23–24)

Love in God's eyes is obedience. We must obey and do what God says.

Now that we know that, how do you love God on your new mission?

It starts with worship.

The Bible calls for worship. It's crucial for the believer. We must worship God.

Worship is any action that magnifies God (makes Him bigger) and makes us smaller.

The book of Psalms is the worship book of the Bible.

Ascribe to the LORD the glory due his name; worship the LORD in the splendor of his holiness. (Psalm 29:2)

The whole earth will worship you and sing praise to you. They will sing praise to your name." Selah (Psalm 66:4)

Come, let us shout joyfully to the LORD, shout triumphantly to the rock of our salvation! (Psalm 95:1)

Come, let us worship and bow down; let us kneel before the LORD our Maker. (Psalm 95:6)

Worship the LORD in the splendor of his holiness; let the whole earth tremble before him. (Psalm 96:9)

HOW DO THESE VERSES FROM PSALMS SAY WE MUST WORSHIP GOD?

When the wise men traveled miles and miles to see Jesus . . .

> *When they saw the star, they were overwhelmed with joy. Entering the house, they saw the child with Mary his mother, and falling to their knees, they worshiped him. Then they opened their treasures and presented him with gifts: gold, frankincense, and myrrh. (Matthew 2:10-11)*

HOW DID THE WISE MEN WORSHIP GOD?

_____

_____

Jesus met a Samaritan woman at a well. She knew a little about the Jewish faith and the Bible. Here's how Jesus told her how to worship.

> *Jesus told her, "Believe me, woman, an hour is coming when you will worship the Father neither on this mountain nor in Jerusalem. You Samaritans worship what you do not know. We worship what we do know, because salvation is from the Jews. But an hour is coming, and is now here, when the true worshipers will worship the Father in Spirit and in truth. Yes, the Father wants such people to worship him." (John 4:21–23)*

HOW DID JESUS TELL THE SAMARITAN WOMAN TO WORSHIP GOD?

How do you make something bigger?

Make yourself smaller.

When John the Baptist saw Jesus, he said these words . . .

"He must increase, but I must decrease." (John 3:30)

How does God increase and you decrease?

For God to get bigger in your life, you have to give more and more of yourself to Him.

Remind yourself:

- What you want is not as important as what God wants
- How you want to spend your time is not as important as where God wants you to spend it
- What you want to say is not as important as what God wants you to say

God must increase in your life. What comes out of you should decrease you and increase God.

In the verses you just read, the Bible revealed to you many ways to worship.

ASCRIBE—give thanks to God when you accomplish something, tell others about His greatness.

SING—listen to and sing worship music.

SHOUT—don't be shy about your love for God.

BOW DOWN/KNEEL—Your body's posture says a lot about your heart when you pray and sing.

TREMBLE—Magnify Him to the point where you see Him as He really is!

GIVE GIFTS—Tithe and give offerings.

SPIRIT—Worship comes from a deeper place inside you. It's not just external actions but internal surrender.

TRUTH—Make sure the things you say and the songs you sing are all based on truth from the Word of God.

Here are some more ways.

PRAYER—When you pray, you acknowledge that God is in control and that there is very little you can do. You submit to Him by surrendering your issues to Him.

BIBLE—When you open the Word of God, God reveals to you His will. His words are more important than your words as you find direction and purpose in the pages.

Be a true worshiper.

Make God increase while you decrease.

Worship not just at church when you sing, but all through your day as you breathe.

Worship God and let others know who has breathed new life into you!

CHAPTER 37

LOVE OTHERS

People can be difficult to love.

When we have problems loving other people, we must remember that God loves us despite all our annoying habits.

> *But God proves his own love for us in that while we were still sinners, Christ died for us. (Romans 5:8)*

If He loves us enough to die for us, can't we at least act nice, respectful, kind, maybe even loving toward others? With your new and improved self, you are equipped to do so.

Ephesians 4–5 reveal some instructions on how to love others.

> *As a prisoner for the Lord, then, I urge you to live a life worthy of the calling you have received. Be completely humble and gentle; be patient, bearing with one another in love. (Ephesians 4:1–2 NIV)*

First, we must BEAR WITH ONE ANOTHER IN LOVE.

What does that mean? Be patient. Be forgiving. Look for the good in someone instead of focusing on the bad.

But this kid picks his nose! BEAR WITH IT IN LOVE.

But this person talks all the time! BEAR WITH IT IN LOVE.

But this girl thinks she's better than everyone! BEAR WITH IT IN LOVE.

But this guy acts embarrassing! BEAR WITH IT IN LOVE.

Ephesians 4 urges us to strive for unity. Making fun of others or gossiping about them destroys that unity we want to build with people who are lost and dying.

Now grace was given to each one of us according to the measure of Christ's gift. (Ephesians 4:7)

We were shown grace so let's show some grace to others. Loving others despite their faults is a sign of maturity. As you grow in God, it gets easier to love with God's love.

Until we all reach unity in the faith and in the knowledge of God's Son, growing into maturity with a stature measured by Christ's fullness. Then we will no longer be little children, tossed by the waves and blown around by every wind of teaching, by human cunning with cleverness in the techniques of deceit. (Ephesians 4:13–14)

Those days of making fun of others are over. Mature Christians sit with the outsiders at lunch, befriend the person everyone mocks.

Think of how many school shootings could have been avoided if the Christians in the school loved the people everyone else laughed at.

Therefore, I say this and testify in the Lord: You should no longer live as the Gentiles live, in the futility of their thoughts. (Ephesians 4:17)

It's tempting to join the crowd and look down on the outsiders because we want to protect our own reputations. Those who torment others are dark, ignorant, callous, and proof of the hardness of their hearts. That's not you, right?

But that is not how you came to know Christ, assuming you heard about him and were taught by him, as the truth is in Jesus, to take off your former way of life, the old self that is corrupted by deceitful desires, to be renewed in the spirit of your minds, and to put on the new self, the one created according to God's likeness in righteousness and purity of the truth. (Ephesians 4:20–24)

You are a different person. You know Christ. You've been taught about Him and know the truth. Strip off that old way of living and toss it in the trash. You are new, created in the likeness of Christ Jesus.

So how do you love others? Ephesians 4–5 goes on to give you a checklist of ways you can love others throughout the day.

- Stop lying (4:25).
- Speak the truth (4:25).
- Be angry without sin (4:26).
- Don't be angry overnight (4:26).
- Do honest work (4:28).
- Don't use foul language (4:29).
- Build up others with what you say (4:29).
- Don't be bitter (4:31).
- Don't slander (4:31).
- Don't hate (4:31).
- Be kind and compassionate (4:32).
- Forgive, because God forgave you (4:32).
- Walk in love (5:2).
- Don't be obscene or crude when you joke (5:4).
- Be thankful (5:4).
- Don't be a part of things that will hurt others (5:11).
- Be smart (5:15).
- Quote Scripture (5:19).
- Submit to one another (5:21).

Try that for one day, being all those things to all the kids at school, at church, and in your neighborhood. See if it doesn't make a difference.

Therefore, be imitators of God, as dearly loved children. (Ephesians 5:1)

BE AN IMITATOR OF GOD!

Do exactly what Jesus would do when He loved others.

SHINE THE LIGHT INTO THE DARKNESS.

Nothing removes darkness faster than light. When true Christ goodness shows up, evil runs away.

For you were once darkness, but now you are light in the Lord. Live as children of light. (Ephesians 5:8)

Ephesians 5:15 goes on to say, "Pay careful attention, then, to how you live . . ." You have to think about every action you do on a regular basis, evaluate your relationship with every person you know or sit by in class or are friends with on social media or who you talk to privately. Are they helping you BE AN IMITATOR OF GOD or making you an imitator of darkness?

How you love others will reveal who you imitate.

Jesus revealed His love to you so go and reveal that love to others!

CHAPTER 38

SHARE THE GOSPEL WITH OTHERS

WHAT WAS THE LAST GOOD NEWS YOU RECEIVED?

_____

_____

WHO DID YOU SHARE IT WITH?

_____

_____

There's lots of good news you probably love to share.

- You made the team.
- You got an A.
- Some girl likes you.
- You got a car.

As you get older, there will be more good news you can't wait to share.

- You got into a college.
- You're getting married.

- Your wife is having a baby.
- You're a grandparent.

People love to hear good news, whether it's their own or others. Good news makes you feel good knowing good things are happening.

Even better, we love to give people good news about their lives. If you saw the roster that you and your best friend made the team, you would run to him and tell him the good news, right?

The word *gospel* comes from a Greek word meaning "good tidings." We also say, "good news." The word is found only in the New Testament.

What's the good news in the Bible?

JESUS CHRIST LOVES YOU AND CAME TO THE EARTH TO DIE FOR YOUR SINS SO YOU CAN HAVE A RELATIONSHIP WITH GOD FOREVER IN ETERNITY!

You are forgiven! You are a new creation! You have hope! You have a purpose!

Come, let us shout joyfully to the LORD, shout trium-phantly to the rock of our salvation! (Psalm 95:1)

There's lots of good news you can receive in this world, but this news is the best by far, hands down, no doubt about it. God has forgiven you of all your sins and you don't ever have to worry about death again. Death is everyone's biggest fear. A relationship with Jesus Christ takes away that fear, and every other fear for that matter.

Why do Christians have to be the ones to spread the gospel?

Jesus told us to.

"And it is necessary that the gospel be preached to all nations." (Mark 13:10)

Then he said to them, "Go into all the world and preach the gospel to all creation." (Mark 16:15)

The book of Acts tells of the apostles doing exactly that. They could not contain the good news and keep it a secret any longer.

So, after they had testified and spoken the word of the Lord, they traveled back to Jerusalem, preaching the gospel in many villages of the Samaritans. (Acts 8:25)

The apostle Paul was driven to share the gospel with everyone he met, even those who hated his guts.

Some Jews came from Antioch and Iconium, and when they won over the crowds, they stoned Paul and dragged him out of the city, thinking he was dead. After the disciples gathered around him, he got up and went into the town. The next day he left with Barnabas for Derbe. (Acts 14:19–20)

Paul went to share the good news. The people thought it was bad news and threw rocks at him, kicking him out of the city. Paul picked himself up and went back into the city that just beat him up. Despite what the people thought, Paul knew this was something they needed to hear.

HOW COMFORTABLE ARE YOU SHARING THE GOSPEL WITH OTHERS?

_____

_____

Jesus told His followers this statement before He departed the earth (UNDERLINE the five things He told us to do):

Jesus came near and said to them, "All authority has been given to me in heaven and on earth. Go, therefore, and make disciples of all nations, baptizing them in the name of the Father and of the Son and of the Holy Spirit, teaching them to observe everything I have commanded you. And remember, I am with you always, to the end of the age." (Matthew 28:18–20)

Find them?

1. Go—follow the path God has laid out for you.

2. Make disciples—share the good news and lead followers to Christ.
3. Baptize them—help them make a public profession of their faith.
4. Teaching them—show them how a Christian lives.
5. Remember—you are not going alone.

You've been sent, so what's stopping you?

CIRCLE AN EXCUSE YOU'VE USED TO NOT SHARE THE GOSPEL.

1. **I don't want to scare someone away from a friendship.**
2. **I don't want others to make fun of me.**
3. **I don't know how to share the gospel.**
4. **What if they ask me questions I can't answer?**

If you circled any of these . . . then you're like everyone else. We've all thought these things, but let's look at some possible answers to these excuses.

1. I don't want to scare someone away from a friendship—but you're okay with your friend going to hell?
2. I don't want others to make fun of me—people made fun of Jesus, so why not you?
3. I don't know how to share the gospel—you can be taught.
4. What if they ask me questions I can't answer—tell them you don't know and go find the answer.

See, every excuse has an answer.

If you don't share the gospel, that's like being ashamed of God. You're embarrassed by Him. And you think He's not right for everyone.

For I am not ashamed of the gospel, because it is the power of God for salvation to everyone who believes, first to the Jew, and also to the Greek. (Romans 1:16)

God is power. God is salvation. God is for everyone.

And God's plan to see salvation come to the world is through His people. You. You are God's billboard, social media post, sky writing message, breaking news, headline.

How can you share the gospel with others?

First, tell your story. It's called a testimony. Your story is good news about how God found you and rescued you.

WRITE OUT YOUR TESTIMONY HERE.

(NOTE: Every testimony has a beginning, middle, and end. Answer these three questions: Who were you before Christ? What happened when you understood the truth about Christ? What's ahead for you now that you know Christ?)

_____

_____

_____

_____

_____

_____

_____

_____

How can anyone deny your testimony? It happened—you were a witness to your own events. Someone may say, "Oh that's good for you." Yes it is. But the Spirit is telling them in their heart, "It's good for you too."

You have to remember that Jesus promised to "be with you always." The Holy Spirit too.

"For the Holy Spirit will teach you at that very hour what must be said." (Luke 12:12)

You're not alone when you carry out the command of sharing the good news. The Holy Spirit is right by your side.

When it comes to explaining the gospel, you can be taught.

There are many ways to share the gospel. If you had to, off the top of your head, on the spot explain the gospel, try this using the most popular verse in the Bible.

For God loved the world in this way: He gave his one and only Son, so that everyone who believes in him will not perish but have eternal life. (John 3:16)

Here are some talking points:

1. God—There is a God, and He created the world and everyone in it. He's eternal, and He knows everything.
2. Loves—God is a loving God. He loves you, and He loves me.
3. The world—He loves everyone in the world, no matter what they've done.
4. He gave—God is giving, and He's willing to give up someone very close to Him.
5. His only Son—Jesus Christ who died on the cross for us, taking on the penalty of our sins so we would not have to suffer any longer and be forgiven.
6. Whoever believes—You must believe. Belief is

more than just knowledge, but total understanding, surrender, and passion.

7. Will not perish—You will die on this earth, but your spirit will never die.

8. Eternal life—If you believe all this, you will live forever with God in eternity.

That's not too hard. There are other ways to share the gospel, but just make sure you talk about JESUS!

You can also try these ways:

- Invite them to church or your youth group.
- Have them talk to your pastor or youth leader.
- Give them a Bible.
- Give them a book (maybe this one).

Once you share, it becomes easier over time. Before long you become a good news machine, sharing everywhere you go.

How beautiful on the mountains
are the feet of the herald,
who proclaims peace,
who brings news of good things,
who proclaims salvation,
who says to Zion, "Your God reigns!" (Isaiah 52:7)

You have the greatest news the world ever needs to hear. Why keep it to yourself? Reveal it to others!

CHAPTER 39

TEACH OTHERS

You know the difference between a good teacher and a bad teacher.

A good teacher makes you want to learn. You relate to the teacher. Sometimes the teacher is honest and open about life. Or the teacher is insightful, making the topics interesting.

A bad teacher . . . A turn-off. Information but no inspiration. And maybe no information.

Remember back in Matthew 28:18–20 when Jesus said, "Go into all the world and make disciples"? That's the part about spreading the good news and seeing people get saved. Once they get saved, they get baptized as a public announcement to everyone.

Now what?

Here's the next part: Teach.

Jesus wants you to be a teacher.

"I'm not a teacher! I can't stand up in front of a bunch of people and talk about God!"

Hold on. Don't forget what we talked about previously—God is with you, the Holy Spirit equips you. You can do all things through Christ who strengthens you. You CAN do it.

But that's not necessarily what a teacher here means. It could be. You may stand in front of a group of people (maybe five year olds or fifteen year olds) and teach them about God (maybe here or another country). It could be twenty people or two people.

The point here is that you are a follower of Jesus Christ and He has in mind some people that He wants you to teach about God. Just be open and available, that's all God asks.

The Bible uses the word *disciple*. A disciple is a student. Matthew 28:18–20 said to "make disciples." Jesus told us to tell people about Him, watch them get saved, and what happens next is that the Holy Spirit makes them hungry for God.

Then Jesus asks that you teach people who want to be taught.

Most teachers in school are assigned to teach students stuff they don't care about. That's a hard job!

You're assigned to teach people stuff they care about.

As a teacher, go find some students who want to learn and teach them more about God, the Bible, truth, life, and Jesus Christ.

When Jesus had finished saying these things, the crowds were amazed at his teaching, because he taught as one who had authority, and not as their teachers of the law. (Matthew 7:28–29 NIV)

Jesus, when He taught, separated Himself from other teachers. When people heard Him they said, "He teaches with authority." What does that mean? It means He knew His material more intimately than other teachers. It was His heart. It was truth. It was really about Himself.

Other teachers quoted Scripture and made points about it, but the people listening could tell it didn't really matter to them.

When you teach, teach with heart. The Word of God must matter to you. Don't say, "Oh, I'm just doing this because God wants me to do this." You should want to make a difference in someone's life. Want to see that person grow and mature in faith. Want to see that disciple go and disciple others.

Therefore you do not lack any spiritual gift as you eagerly wait for our Lord Jesus Christ to be revealed. (1 Corinthians 1:7 NIV)

There are some things called *spiritual gifts*. When you get saved, the Holy Spirit comes and lives inside you. He brings with Him all His characteristics to spread the good news. Some of those qualities are intensified in some and highlighted to different degrees.

There are a number of spiritual gifts mentioned in the Bible—serving, giving, administration, faith, evangelizing. One of them is teaching. So should only those who have that gift of teaching, teach?

Those with the gift of teaching will want to teach and nobody can stop them. When they teach, they will have an easier time because they can feel the Spirit flowing through them.

However, we're all called to teach someone, but how you teach will be different than others.

Some will stand at the podium and teach thousands.

Others will gather some friends at lunch and talk about the Bible.

Some will use their own words and insight in a blog.

Others will use a video to teach while they conclude by asking questions.

It's doesn't matter how. It does matter if you don't.

Another excuse is building in your mind. "What if the people ask hard questions and I don't know the answer?"

Teach with humility. Don't pretend you know everything and have mastered everything. Those teachers that Jesus argued with (the Pharisees) thought they knew everything until they encountered God.

If someone asks you a hard question, it's not a problem to say, "Hmmm, I don't know the answer to that. I'll get you the answer next time we get together."

Then go ask a pastor or student leader or use a Bible search tool to see other verses about the same topic.

You have so many resources at your fingertips. You can become an expert quickly.

This next part is hard, I'll admit. Teach by example.

A disciple is not above his teacher, but everyone who is fully trained will be like his teacher. (Luke 6:40)

As a teacher, you present yourself as someone who is trying to live by what you are teaching. It is an expectation. If you teach about sexual purity, then make out with a girl in the hallway, people will wonder if what you teach really matters.

Living up to the example you teach is hard. The example is Jesus Christ. You are teaching others how to live like Christ. You must do the same.

Teach with passion and boldness.

Every day in the temple, and in various homes, they continued teaching and proclaiming the good news that Jesus is the Messiah. (Acts 5:42)

The early followers of Christ taught every chance they got. They saw the difference they were making in people's lives. They faced opposition, getting thrown into jail, stoned, and chased out of town.

Be ready. Maybe you won't get chased out of town, but kids will make fun of those who pray around a pole, or open a Bible in the cafeteria, or wear a Jesus T-shirt.

It happened to Jesus, why wouldn't it happen to you? Let the opposition fuel your energy to stand up and keep going. Don't let it stop you; let it motivate you.

Teach with patience. Seeing results takes time. It took three years for Peter to finally get it right. Then Peter stood in front of 3,000 people and delivered an incredible message, the first sermon about Jesus ever spoken.

Paul would go into towns and stay awhile.

He stayed there a year and a half, teaching the word of God among them. (Acts 18:11)

Paul stayed two whole years in his own rented house. And he welcomed all who visited him, proclaiming the kingdom of God and teaching about the Lord Jesus Christ with all boldness and without hindrance. (Acts 28:30–31)

You can't disciple someone for one week and expect to see a difference. Part of Jesus' discipleship tactic was living with His apostles for three years, 24/7. There will come a time, though, when you need to leave and let them find their own disciples to teach.

And don't forget this: teach with the Bible. Even books like the one you're reading now should always be used in partnership with God's Word, never in place of it.

No builder enters a work site without tools. No soldier enters a war zone without a weapon. You have a tool that's also a weapon—the Word of God.

All Scripture is inspired by God and is profitable for teaching, for rebuking, for correcting, for training in righteousness, so that the man of God may be complete, equipped for every good work. (2 Timothy 3:16–17)

The Word of God does all the work. It . . .

- Teaches
- Rebukes
- Corrects
- Trains
- Equips

You just have to read it, ask questions, talk about it, apply it. Every time you teach, the Word of God must be somewhere in your lesson plan.

Let's end on this sobering thought. It's scary, but it needs to be said.

If you're a teacher, know that there's a stricter judgment on you than someone who isn't a teacher.

Not many should become teachers, my brothers, because you know that we will receive a stricter judgment. (James 3:1)

If you tell other people how to live, and don't live that way, God grades your life on a tougher curve. You have to live up to what you are teaching.

Don't let this scare you away from teaching, but motivate you to live better.

You have to live up to what you're teaching. While there's a greater curve you're judged by, there's also a greater blessing you receive.

Embrace the challenge. Find a few people your age and start a Bible study. Or find a new Christian and help him with his new walk with Christ.

A teacher taught you about Jesus. It's time to reveal to others what you know.

CHAPTER 40

SERVE OTHERS

In tennis, the opening shot is called a serve. It begins a volley of back and forth that goes until someone messes up. When you serve, you're sending the ball to the other person.

Serving in life is sort of like tennis. It's not competitive, the goal isn't to get someone to mess up, but it's like tennis in that you have to take the initiative and go first, and when you do, it sparks more serving in others. (Plus, you should serve your enemies even if they're out to beat you.)

We could list a hundred ways to serve others and take up lots of page space, but we won't. Let's just define it.

SERVING: Any way you help another person, anywhere you are.

That definition is pretty clear and simple. It starts at home, continues to friends, extends to school, and goes out into the world.

Serving requires your attention to matters around you (not just yourself and your needs) and dropping what you're doing to lend a hand to someone in need.

It's pretty clear what serving is; the big question is how to serve.

For even the Son of Man did not come to be served,
but to serve, and to give his life as a ransom for many."
(Mark 10:45)

Jesus' primary purpose for coming to Earth was to serve. He didn't expect power, prestige, or notoriety. He didn't expect a single person to lift a finger to help Him. His serving didn't come with an expectation.

He served to show His love to others. We must serve to reveal God's love to others.

How you serve makes all the difference. Let's look at the story that led up to the Mark 10:45 "Jesus came to serve" verse.

Then James and John, the sons of Zebedee, came to him.
"Teacher," they said, "we want you to do for us whatever
we ask." (Mark 10:35 NIV)

"What do you want me to do for you?" he asked. (Mark
10:36 NIV)

They replied, "Let one of us sit at your right and the
other at your left in your glory." (Mark 10:37 NIV)

By this time in Jesus' ministry, the apostles felt Jesus came to defeat the Romans and take back Israel. They knew He was from God, but they were unclear about His mission. They looked for their angle, what they could get out of all this.

"You don't know what you are asking," Jesus said. "Can you drink the cup I drink or be baptized with the baptism I am baptized with?"

"We can," they answered.

Jesus said to them, "You will drink the cup I drink and be baptized with the baptism I am baptized with, but to sit at my right or left is not for me to grant. These places belong to those for whom they have been prepared." (Mark 10:38–40 NIV)

Jesus used the word *baptized* to mean "fully immersed." He was fully immersed in a mission and a cause and headed to death because of it. He challenged these two by saying, "Are you all-in and willing to die?" James and John agreed.

The others weren't too excited by what they heard.

When the ten heard about this, they became indignant with James and John. Jesus called them together and said, "You know that those who are regarded as rulers of the Gentiles lord it over them, and their high officials exercise authority over them. Not so with you. Instead, whoever wants to become great among you must be your servant, and whoever wants to be first must be slave of all." (Mark 10:41–44 NIV)

People don't like it when you try to push ahead and get more out of life than them. Jesus used this opportunity to teach about attitude when serving. He said non-Christians like being rulers, like being in charge, like it when others see them as being the boss. But not so with Christians. No, they lead a different way.

Christians don't lead for authority. Christians lead out of humility.

God sees greatness in those who put themselves last and others first—those who get at the end of the line so others can get fed first—who consider their needs inconsequential and others more important.

The only time in the Gospels you see Jesus ever doing something for Himself was praying, and even then He got up early before anyone was awake or needed Him for something.

This is where verse 45 drops in.

"For even the Son of Man did not come to be served, but to serve, and to give his life as a ransom for many." (Mark 10:45 NIV)

Look, if God came to Earth to serve, not expecting anyone to lift a finger for Him, why should you expect others to wait on you?

The Bible gives us other tips on how to serve like Jesus. In Ephesians 6, Paul speaks to those who are slaves or servants, communicating a principle we can apply to any job.

Slaves, obey your earthly masters with respect and fear, and with sincerity of heart, just as you would obey

Christ. Obey them not only to win their favor when their eye is on you, but as slaves of Christ, doing the will of God from your heart. Serve wholeheartedly, as if you were serving the Lord, not people, because you know that the Lord will reward each one for whatever good they do, whether they are slave or free. (Ephesians 6:5–8 NIV)

How are we supposed to serve?

- Respectfully
- Fearfully
- Sincerely
- Obediently
- Wholeheartedly

We are to serve people here on Earth—parents, teachers, bosses, church leaders—as if we were running an errand, or washing his car, or cleaning up our room for God.

We should also serve without receiving credit and without expecting anything in return. You're serving the Lord, remember. He's watching and taking notes.

And we're not supposed to treat people differently; whether they are a believer or not.

All who are under the yoke of slavery should consider their masters worthy of full respect, so that God's name and our teaching may not be slandered. Those who have believing masters should not show them disrespect just because they are fellow believers. Instead, they should serve them even better because their masters are dear to them as fellow believers and are devoted to the welfare of their slaves. (1 Timothy 6:1–2 NIV)

Being a slave back then meant you had no rights. Paul said this to slaves, telling them to serve their believing masters as well as their unbelieving masters. Paul frequently referred to himself as a servant of God, a slave in chains. He saw himself as one who had no rights. He didn't see himself deserving a promotion or extra money in his paycheck.

He put himself in the worst possible situations to be an example for Christ no matter what the cost.

We end with one more thought from Paul

Be devoted to one another in love. Honor one another above yourselves. Never be lacking in zeal, but keep your spiritual fervor, serving the Lord. Be joyful in hope, patient in affliction, faithful in prayer. (Romans 12:10–12 NIV)

Serving is not a game. It's not a competition. You're not trying to win.

Serving is helping someone else so that they can win and being totally fine with coming in last.

Remember . . .

Jesus did not come to be served, but to serve.

CHAPTER 41

WALK IN THE SPIRIT

Have you ever thought about the way you walk?

Do you drag your feet?

Do you strut with style?

Do you enter a room with attitude?

Are you flat-footed or pigeon-toed?

Most people don't think about their walk until someone points it out.

"Hey, you walk funny."

Then we think about it and try to correct it, but eventually we'll just slip back into our walking routine.

The Bible talks about our "walk." It doesn't mean a casual stroll through the neighborhood. Our walk is the way we conduct ourselves everywhere we go. It's where we are physically present and making an impact. It's the place where you take Christ.

We discussed earlier that the Holy Spirit lives inside you. You carry around the Spirit and walk Him to school, to church, to home, to your friend's house, to the store.

Walking in the Spirit means more than transportation. Walking in the Spirit means transformation.

The Spirit transforms your walk—not with attitude, but humility. You walk around life a totally different person and carry the message of Christ by who you are.

You need to shower daily, sometimes twice. Put on deodorant. Body sprays. And make sure you wear clean clothes because they soak up your smell.

Guess what, if you stink, people don't want to be around you. Nothing personal, you just offend their noses.

When you walk with the Spirit, you carry a certain aroma also.

> *But thanks be to God, who always leads us in Christ's triumphal procession and through us spreads the **aroma** of the knowledge of him in every place. For to God we are the **fragrance** of Christ among those who are being saved and among those who are perishing. To some we are an **aroma** of death leading to death, but to others, an **aroma** of life leading to life. Who is adequate for these things? (2 Corinthians 2:14–16)*

If someone smells good, it's pleasant to be around them.

If someone acts like Christ, people like to be around them. People liked to be around Jesus. He attracted HUGE crowds. He carried an aroma of love, forgiveness, acceptance, security, and healing.

So draw people to Christ by the way you carry yourself and how you live your life.

As a Christian, there are two ways to walk—in the FLESH or in the SPIRIT. Your body battles between going one way or the other.

I say then, walk by the Spirit and you will certainly not carry out the desire of the flesh. For the flesh desires what is against the Spirit, and the Spirit desires what is against the flesh; these are opposed to each other, so that you don't do what you want. (Galatians 5:16–17)

Where the Spirit wants to take you is totally different than where the flesh wants to take you. The Spirit listens to God (because He is God). The flesh listens to the world. How do you do that? Paul laid out a walking plan in Romans 8.

Therefore, there is now no condemnation for those in Christ Jesus, because the law of the Spirit of life in Christ Jesus has set you free from the law of sin and death. (vv. 1–2)

With every step you take, remember this: You are free! You don't have to impress anybody. God set you free, and you are going to walk right into heaven one day.

What the law could not do since it was weakened by the flesh, God did. He condemned sin in the flesh by sending his own Son in the likeness of sinful flesh as a sin offering, in order that the law's requirement would be fulfilled in us who do not walk according to the flesh but according to the Spirit. (vv. 3–4)

Jesus was born in the flesh, walked around in the flesh, then successfully triumphed over the flesh by never sinning. He's the only one in the history of the world ever to do so. He lived as the only perfect person ever.

The law was created for fleshly people like us to guide us to godliness. We fail miserably, while Jesus won victoriously.

Jesus saved us from the inside (the Spirit), to help us succeed on the outside (flesh). Now we can walk like Jesus according to the Spirit.

> *For those who live according to the flesh have their minds set on the things of the flesh, but those who live according to the Spirit have their minds set on the things of the Spirit. Now the mind-set of the flesh is death, but the mind-set of the Spirit is life and peace. The mind-set of the flesh is hostile to God because it does not submit to God's law. Indeed, it is unable to do so. (vv. 5–7)*

Here's the key to walking in the Spirit. Setting our minds.

Before Christ, we just did what our flesh told us to do. We naturally did what our sinful flesh wanted.

NO MORE! It's time to retrain our thinking to behave according to the Spirit.

FLESH: Hey, that girl's hot.   SPIRIT: Hey, pray for that girl.

FLESH: That kid's weird.   SPIRIT: Go talk to that kid.

FLESH: My parents know nothing.   SPIRIT: God gave me my parents.

FLESH: Let's look at porn.   SPIRIT: Let's not.

See the difference? You have to stop letting the flesh run the show. It's time for the Spirit to take over your mind and communicate through actions.

> *Those who are in the flesh cannot please God. You, however, are not in the flesh, but in the Spirit, if indeed the Spirit of God lives in you. If anyone does not have the Spirit of Christ, he does not belong to him. Now if Christ is in you, the body is dead because of sin, but the Spirit gives life because of righteousness. (vv. 8–10)*

Your flesh (body) has no power over you. It's dead. But you can continue to allow the flesh to have power if you allow it to take charge. You have the ability to walk by the Spirit. Use it! Think about it!

> *And if the Spirit of him who raised Jesus from the dead lives in you, then he who raised Christ from the dead will also bring your mortal bodies to life through his Spirit who lives in you. (v. 11)*

You have the same amount of power that raised Jesus from the dead. Now reveal Jesus to the world by the way you walk through life.

Rise up, Spirit! Take over. Walk like Christ wherever you go!

CHAPTER 42

GO ON MISSION

One more question to ask you: where are you going?

I don't mean after you put this book down, but where are you going in your life?

Yogi Berra, an old-time baseball player, once said: *"If you don't know where you are going, you'll end up someplace else."* Funny, right?

Without a plan, you wander, unsure about yourself, and doubting God.

A mission is an adventure with purpose. Those who go on a mission know exactly where they are going. Now it wouldn't be an adventure without challenges and forced detours. You can overcome those obstacles, change your strategy, and get back to the mission.

We're going to get deep here. Sit back and pray about this one. Think carefully.

WHERE DO YOU WANT TO BE IN FIVE YEARS?

_____

_____

WHERE DO YOU WANT TO BE IN TEN YEARS?

_____

_____

WHERE DO YOU WANT TO BE IN FIFTY YEARS?

_____

_____

These goals help you walk every day through life with purpose. Every decision you make will determine how you arrive at that future destination.

Jesus gave His apostles a mission. In Matthew 28:18–20, Jesus told them to go into all the world, make disciples, baptize them, and teach them. That was a general mission. Each apostle had his own specific part of that mission.

Peter's mission was similar to Andrew (his brother), but different than James or John. Philip went on different missions than Thomas. Paul took on Asia, establishing churches all throughout Greece and the area known today as Turkey. He took Barnabas with him for some of it, but Barnabas branched off and started his own mission adventures.

God designed you for a mission. You may work alongside others or take off on your own. You may reach people in your city or in a distant country.

In Acts 1, we see the final departure of Jesus as He ascended into heaven. Before He left, Jesus gave the apostles encouragement and more details on the mission. In Matthew 28, Jesus detailed WHAT the mission was (make, baptize, teach). In Acts 1, we read the WHERE and HOW that mission will be accomplished.

> *"But you will receive power when the Holy Spirit has come on you, and you will be my witnesses in Jerusalem, in all Judea and Samaria, and to the end of the earth."*
> *(Acts 1:8)*

WHERE: Jerusalem, Judea, Samaria, the ends of the earth

HOW: By the power of the Holy Spirit

The where of Jesus' mission describes concentric circles of influence. Think of it this way.

JERUSALEM is the local area where you live, the dot on the center of the map. "You are here!" It's your hometown, school, church. Then a little wider out . . .

JUDEA is the surrounding area with people like you. It's your whole city, people outside your school, but in your school district, maybe your county. Then a little wider out . . .

SAMARIA is the area where people live not like you. A different color maybe, or a different economic class. They could be in your city or outside your city or outside your state or a different part of the United States. They aren't good or bad, just people with different ways of doing things. Then a little wider out . . .

ENDS OF THE EARTH are all the nations outside your own, foreign nations where you need a passport to get to.

Jesus said your mission may take you to all these places. Will He take you to all these places? Not sure. But are you available to go to all these places? That's the real question.

After Jesus gave His apostles the final details of the mission, He ascended into heaven. Then the Bible says . . .

After he had said this, he was taken up as they were watching, and a cloud took him out of their sight. While he was going, they were gazing into heaven, and suddenly two men in white clothes stood by them. They said, "Men of Galilee, why do you stand looking up into heaven? This same Jesus, who has been taken from you into heaven, will come in the same way that you have seen him going into heaven." (Acts 1:9–11)

We don't know how long they stood there gazing, but it was long enough that two angels needed to enter the scene and say, "Why are you standing around? Jesus told you what to do and He's coming back . . . someday. Let's go!"

Those angels could have said that to the church today: "Don't stand around. Now it's your turn to carry out what Jesus has revealed to you."

You see, we can be told what to do, but then we have to do it.

Are you standing around waiting for something to drop out of the sky? Do you need more information?

You know God created you in the womb with a specific purpose in mind.

You know you've sinned against God.

You know God saved you through Jesus Christ, making you completely new.

You know you have a new identity in Christ.

The Bible revealed all that to you.

So, GO. Get moving. Pray. Start things. Get organized.

Discover God's plan for you as you go, not before you go.

The orders are to GO and BE like Christ. Along the way, the Holy Spirit reveals more information.

Every day is a mission trip. Are you ready for your life adventure?

CHAPTER 43

LIVE OUT YOUR IDENTITY

Imagine if Superman never revealed his true identity. He stayed as Clark Kent all the time, acting like a reporter and reporting all the news but never jumping in and saving people from death.

A waste, right?

You have a new identity. You are made in the likeness of Jesus Christ, who lived as the greatest Super Man ever. That identity is inside of you. You need to reveal to the world who you really are, and what you were made to do.

You've looked at all the evidence, asked the hard questions, and made decisions along the way.

God has revealed to you the truth through His Word, His Holy Spirit, and through others around you.

This investigation has changed your life, your direction, and your identity.

Now live it out.

NOTES

1. https://ghr.nlm.nih.gov/primer/basics/dna
2. You can check the current world population here: http://www.worldometers.info/world-population/
3. https://www.baumanmedical.com/qa/many-hairs-human-head/
4. As of January 2019: http://www.worldometers.info/world-population/
5. https://spaceplace.nasa.gov/review/dr-marc-space/solar-systems-in-galaxy.html
6. Strong's H930
7. https://www.blueletterbible.org/lang/lexicon/lexicon.cfm?Strongs=H930&t=KJV
8. Strongs H3882
9. https://www.blueletterbible.org/lang/lexicon/lexicon.cfm?Strongs=H3882&t=KJV
10. https://www.huffpost.com/entry/healthy-relationships_b_3307916
11. I'm way underestimating the actual number but trying to make a point.
12. https://www.lawserver.com/law/state/arizona/az-laws/arizona_laws_3-2664
13. https://leginfo.legislature.ca.gov/faces/codes_displaySection.xhtml?lawCode=FGC&sectionNum=6883.&article=2.&highlight=true&keyword=frog
14. https://www.courant.com/news/connecticut/hc-xpm-1996-02-14-9602140505-story.html
15. https://www.isustudentmedia.com/indiana_statesman/opinion/columns/article_519941e8-5702-11e5-9b55-f711898b1b45.html
16. https://loweringthebar.net/2011/09/greased-pig-contests-illegal-in-minnesota.html
17. https://abovethelaw.com/2015/03/criminally-yours-your-one-phone-call/
18. http://www.mirandawarning.org/whatareyourmirandarights.html
19. Romans 3:23
20. Romans 5:8

21. Romans 6:23

22. Romans 8:1

23. Romans 8:38–39

24. Romans 10:9

25. Romans 10:13

26. https://www.distancecalculator.net/from-los-angeles-to-new-york-city

27. https://novaonline.nvcc.edu/eli/evans/his241/notes/geography/geography.html

28. https://mars.nasa.gov/allaboutmars/nightsky/mars-close-approach/

29. www.dictionary.com

30. www.dictionary.com

31. www.dictionary.com

32. https://www.bjs.gov/index.cfm?ty=pbdetail&iid=6266

33. https://bible.org/illustration/pharisaic-laws

34. https://www.archdaily.com/779178/these-are-the-worlds-25-tallest-buildings

35. https://theskydeck.com/the-tower/facts-about-the-ledge/

36. https://www.healthline.com/health/list-of-phobias

37. https://www.blueletterbible.org/lang/lexicon/lexicon.cfm?Strongs=G2716&t=KJV